GUS H. SMALL

THE BANK IS NOT YOUR FRIEND

A SMALL BUSINESS OWNER'S GUIDE
TO FINANCIAL SURVIVAL DURING
GOOD AND BAD TIMES

ISBN 978-1-66780-849-9 (Print)

ISBN 978-1-66780-850-5 (eBook)

For Patty

You have been my life partner
and love for over 50 years

TABLE OF CONTENTS

DISCLAIMER

This Book is not a legal treatise, but a collection of observations and opinions made by the author based on over fifty years of practicing law. Neither the author, nor the publisher of this Book intends to give, or is giving legal advice to the reader.

Actions taken by the reader in response to passages or anything else contained in this Book should not be taken without consulting a licensed attorney at law in the jurisdiction where the reader will be taking such action.

The author makes no warranties of any kind as to his opinions or any other contents of this Book.

Put simply, if you or your business is having financial difficulties, employ a competent attorney skilled in commercial law and bankruptcy.

INTRODUCTION

For over five decades, I have represented small businesses and entrepreneurs in troubled financial situations. I have also represented numerous creditors, both secured and unsecured. In the last thirty years, I have represented far more borrowers and small businesses than I have creditors, probably because banks and other lenders gravitate these days to the larger law firms rather than to boutiques such as my firm. This wasn't the case years ago, as you will see in Chapter 10 when I discuss one of my mentors.

These small businesses have assets ranging from several hundred thousand dollars to tens of millions of dollars. Many of my clients were undercapitalized, made unfortunate financial decisions like expanding too fast, or they simply were undercapitalized in a down market and were just victims of bad economic times. In many cases they waited too long before seeking help. All were being pushed by their lenders and vendors.

In some instances, we were able resolve the creditor issues through negotiations and settlement. Other times we were forced to litigate in court or to file Chapter 11 bankruptcy for our client. Finally, in some cases, the only resolution was to liquidate the company's assets, either out of court or through bankruptcy.

Over the years the nature and methodology of financial workouts have changed. For example, during the Great Recession, new players emerged like the Federal Deposit Insurance Corporation ("FDIC") and equity funds and other parties which had partnerships with the FDIC. These equity funds and other parties purchased bad loans from the FDIC as did some larger and even smaller banks. Other banks bought failed banks and their loan portfolios from the FDIC.

There were, and still are numerous "bottom feeders," debt-buyers who bought, and continue to buy bad loans from banks, credit card companies and other lenders at huge discounts. Dealing with these new types of lenders was and continues to be challenging for borrowers and their attorneys, to say the least.

In representing troubled small businesses, the adverse effect of personal guarantees and the potential loss of personal assets such as the owner's residence always are factors to consider when attempting a small-business workout. In recent times these problems have been exacerbated by the Great Recession and the Covid Pandemic.

When the value of real estate and other assets plummeted in the Great Recession it created an extraordinary burden on small and large real estate developers, long pillars of our economy. While eagerly taking government bailouts, banks turned their backs on these entrepreneurs by refusing to renew their loans or to agree to reasonable settlements.[1] A thirty-year relationship with a bank and a course of dealing, including renewals, meant nothing in those days. I was there consoling my clients who just could not understand why they were being mistreated by the very banks for which they had made so much money over so many years.

Finally, in the recent days of Covid-19, many small businesses in especially affected industries like the hospitality and travel industries have been seriously hurt by the pandemic. Unfortunately, while Covid-19 government grants and loans have helped many businesses, it has also created a new

---

1 I remember attending a dinner at the beginning of the bank bail-out. The speaker was the president of one of the local banks. He first emphasized that his bank did not need, and really didn't want the bail-out money. He then said that the bank would use these funds to expand its business. He said nothing about any intent to help small businesses who owed money to the bank. As it turned out later, the FDIC determined that his bank was really in bad shape. It would have failed but for the bailout money. Of course, there was no bailout money for borrowers, who often asked me, "where is my bailout money?"

kind of business entity, the "Zombie Company," a company which survives only because the government is pumping in funds and/or its lenders are not enforcing their default rights. A zombie company is not viable and has no future, but for the governmental cash infusions. It was and is a candidate for a liquidation either out of court or in bankruptcy. Unfortunately, my experience is that the government bailouts simply lengthen the moment of reckoning for the zombies and make it much more difficult for the owners of these companies to survive financially because of their personal guarantee obligations.

Banks for many years have advertised that they are their customer's partner and friend. I was recently with one of my sons who had to go to the bank to transact some business. I went with him and waited in the lobby. As I looked around, I saw a large billboard attached to one of the walls with a graphic whose purpose was obviously to show the relationship between the bank and its borrowers. Among the many words and phrases on the graphic were *loyalty, partnership, friendship, "building a better future together"* and *"support the financial wellness of small business."* If the banks were ever a small business owner's partner or friend, they definitely are not anymore, and probably never were. Ask any small businessperson who has been through hard times to tell you how their dealings with banks and other lenders changed from the beginning of their relationship to the point where they were near or in default of their loan obligations, or just wanted to renew their loans.

I started writing bits and pieces of this Book right after the Great Recession ended. Many of my borrower clients suffered financially through no fault of their own. In my view the real fault during those hard years lay with the failure of Congress, federal agencies and state legislatures to protect small businesses from greedy banks and other unscrupulous lenders and securities brokers. Some blame is also shouldered by judges in many federal and state courts who were faced with an avalanche of commercial litigation and simply did not understand commercial law and the practical effect of their decisions.[2]

I have written this Book primarily to educate you, the small business owners and entrepreneurs on how the creditor's rights and debtor relief system works so that you can protect yourselves when dealing with your bank and your other creditors. Even though small businesses and their owners are the backbone of this country, they are usually forgotten by state and federal legislators, who write the laws and rules governing the relationships between creditors and debtors. It is therefore not surprising that the banks and other lenders have such an unreasonable leverage in the debtor-creditor relationship.[3]

I have found that my small business clients have a great deal of knowledge about their businesses, but unfortunately not very much knowledge about what happens when they have financial difficulties or even how the law governs their relationships with banks and vendors in their particular industry. I hope this Book will help the small business owners and entrepreneurs to flourish in good times and to survive in bad times. I am also hopeful that this Book may help lawyers who are general practitioners or who practice in areas other than the commercial and bankruptcy area. Finally, professionals like accountants and others who are not business owners may obtain some benefit from the material I have covered.

I have included a primer course on the legal principals governing the system. I explain how small businesses are structured, how bankruptcy

---

2 In my opinion there are too many former prosecutors who are appointed or elected to judgeships who have little or no experience in or understanding of commercial law. Some of these judges are just downright ignorant with respect to complicated commercial law issues. On the other hand, most Bankruptcy Judges, especially those who come from commercial practices, are extremely knowledgeable in commercial law. But a small business or its owners must file bankruptcy to get the benefit of these judges!

3 I do not disagree with the concept that the law should favor the ability of a lender to get its loan repaid by its borrower or from its borrower's assets. I do oppose laws and litigation procedures which permit a lender to require a borrower to *waive* important rights such as surety and equitable defenses, all of which protect the borrower from lender negligence. I also oppose laws and litigation procedures which allow a lender to avoid crediting the true value of its collateral against a borrower's indebtedness if it is going to liquidate the collateral. The sue first and foreclose later methodology is especially unfair.

law, including Chapter 11 works and I discuss litigation and so-called asset protection. I also discuss various types of loans and personal guarantees and what happens when they go bad. During my discussion of these principals, I have given the reader hypotheticals and even some real-life examples of cases in which I served as counsel for the borrower and guarantors. Of course, I protect the identity of my clients by changing the names or not using names at all and in some instances tweaking the facts. I also suggest strategies to follow.

Besides the joy of summarizing the substance of over fifty years of my practice by just writing this Book, I have enjoyed including my opinions regarding how federal and state governments have mistreated small businesses and entrepreneurs in favor of making the creditor rights/debtor relief laws patently unfair. As will become clear as you read this Book, these unfair laws enable lenders and vendors to brutalize borrowers or customers who are having financial difficulties and to force them into bankruptcy. I have also included my opinions on what I also view as unfair and sometimes stupid actions taken by banks and other lenders. As I have told many borrower clients, I have made a nice living over many years dealing with decisions made by inept bankers.

That is not to say that all banks and bankers are inept or deal unfairly with their troubled borrowers. I have represented many lenders who moderate their desire to maximize recovery of a bad debt with empathy, reasonableness and fairness. In fact, I discuss in Chapter 10 on workouts my working relationship with a Special Assets senior banker in a very large bank who turned out, unknowingly, to be one of my mentors. It is important to note that many banks have other departments dealing in wills and trusts and securities. The bankers in these departments have nothing to do with loans to small businesses, and these bankers are just as skilled in their professional activities as are persons in other businesses. I offer no opinions on these bankers, and nothing in this Book is meant to cast any aspersions against them.

Finally, it is my hope that I will help small businesses and entrepreneurs to level the playing field with banks, vendors and other lenders.

Gus H. Small September 2021

THE STRUCTURE OF THE MODERN SMALL BUSINESS

Partnerships and Proprietorships

General Partnerships

When I first got out of the Army and started practicing law, I joined a law firm which was a general partnership. This was the accepted structure of law firms and many businesses at that time. A few years later when I became a junior partner, I realized that under the law I was 100% liable for all of the debts of the partnership, although my ownership percentage of the firm was in the low single digits. We had thirty-five lawyers and a like number of staff. My personal monthly exposure was way more than the total of what I would earn in my first several years as a partner!

When businessmen and women decide to become "partners" in a business, sometimes they decide to form a general partnership.[4] This structure, while not prevalent in recent years, is still found in farming communities and in some small family businesses. Many times, there is no

---

4 A senior federal judge once opined that the worse kind of "ship" is a partnership. It leaves the port in great shape, and then when the partners start disagreeing, it can sink rapidly.

partnership agreement, and the agreement is oral even as to what percentage each "partner" owns.

As is clear from my personal exposure as a junior general partner, **a general partnership is a business structure that must be avoided**. It is dangerous because the law makes the owners liable, jointly and severally, for **all of the debts** of the partnership, even when those debts are not personally guaranteed. With so many modern-day choices of how to structure a small business, there is, in my opinion, no reason ever to structure a business as a general partnership. The tax benefits can easily be obtained using other structures such as limited liability companies and "S-corporations."

Unfortunately, many small businesspeople do not even know that they are using a general partnership because they have no agreement in writing. As indicated above, two or more individuals can form a general partnership orally which is enforceable. For example, if Aunt Sally and Sally's brother, Uncle George, own a grocery store, and they don't have a written partnership agreement, they have formed an oral general partnership by default which is enforceable against them under the law. What ownership percentage each owns will have to be decided by a judge or jury if there is ever a dispute—unless they have a written contract providing for different percentages of ownership.

The real risk is what will happen when one of them dies, and his or her heirs inherit their parent's grocery store interest. George's heirs may not like or trust Sally's family. Don't let this happen to you or your family. Form some other business structure like a limited liability partnership or corporation. They are easy and cheap to set up, and any general practice lawyer can economically take care of the details. In fact, in many states, you can set these entities up yourself online.

Limited Partnership

The Limited Partnership ("LP") was the precursor of the Limited Liability Company ("LLC") and the Limited Liability Partnership ("LLP").

All of the states have statutes governing LP's. In the LP there are limited partners who are like shareholders of a corporation in that they are not liable for the debts of the LP unless they personally guarantee the debts, **or**, importantly, unless they actively engage in the management of the LP. The LP is run by a **general partner** who *is* liable for all of the debts of the LP.

Years ago, the general partner might have been an individual. In recent times, the general partner has been a limited liability shell entity or corporation. Because of the availability of the newer structures like limited liability partnerships and limited liability companies, LPs are seldom used anymore as a business structure, but they are still around.

Limited Liability Partnerships

Limited Liability Partnerships ("LLP's") are very recent business structures permitted by most, but not all states. You, Aunt Sally and Uncle George can form an LLP in which the three of you are still partners, but your liability is limited to your investment in the company, and unless any of you personally guarantee a debt of the LLP, you are not individually liable. Any or all of the three of you can be the managers or operators of the LLP without fear of losing your limited liability. There are downsides to LLP's—especially when they experience financial difficulties. We will discuss this at the end of this Chapter.

Many law firms which previously used a general partnership structure now have converted to limited liability partnerships.

Limited Liability Companies

Another recent form of incorporation is the Limited Liability Company ("LLC"), which is an authorized business entity in all of the fifty states and the District of Columbia. Depending on the state statute, the Limited Liability Company is very similar to a corporation in that it has investors which are called "members" rather than shareholders, and it has a "manager" rather than a CEO, although in recent times, many LLC's have officers, and some even have a board of directors. Neither the members, nor the manager—and there can be more than one manager—are liable for the debts of the LLC unless they personally guarantee the debts. In fact, the LLC can be "member managed" and not have a manager at all. As in the case of the LLP, there are significant downsides to the LLC structure if the LLC suffers financial difficulties.

Proprietorships

The time-honored structure for a business owned by just one individual is the proprietorship. This business is the owner, and the owner is the business. There is no incorporation or partnership agreement. The owner obtains whatever business license is required by the local government and starts operating. No tax return is required since the owner can simply show the income and expenses on his or her personal return. Unfortunately, as in the case of the general partnership, the owner of a proprietorship is one hundred percent liable for all of the debts of the proprietorship.

I once had a client who owned his business as a proprietorship tell me that he never had to guarantee any of the business' bank or vendor debt. He was very proud of that fact, that is, until I told him that there was no need for the bank or the vendors to require him to personally guarantee the debts because as a proprietorship, he was individually liable for all of them anyway.

As in the case of the general partnership, this type of business structure is also to be avoided.

Corporations

Most every businessperson knows about corporations. They have been around for a very long time. The garden variety small business corporation has shareholders who are the owners, a board of directors who elect the officers of the corporation and various officers who run it. Neither the shareholders nor the officers and directors are liable for the debts of the corporation unless they personally guarantee the debts.

Unfortunately, many small businesses who operate under a corporate structure, ignore the formal requirements of keeping corporate books and records which contain the share certificates issued to the owners, corporate minutes and corporate resolutions. In a small business corporation, these generally are things that the owner(s) can do themselves through online forms or by asking their accountant or lawyer to help them prepare these necessary forms. Keeping these books and records is really very easy for a small business, and the failure to do so can be problematical.

Besides ignoring the formalities of keeping separate books and records, some small business owners simply treat their corporate entity— and that includes all the other forms providing limited liability—as a personal "piggy bank" by paying personal debts out of corporate funds and using the corporate bank account as if it was their own. In recent years, we are seeing more and more creditors suing individual shareholders on the theory that the individuals and the corporation are *alter egos*. We will discuss *alter ego* claims in Chapter 12 and how negligently (or purposely) treating the corporation as a personal piggy bank can result in making the owner liable for all of the debts of the corporation.[5]

Tax Issues with Entities

The government in recent years has permitted the shareholders of a corporation, the members of an LLC or the partners in other types of limited liability partnerships to decide how they want to be taxed. Generally, the election is made when the company is formed or starts business. Thus, no matter what the entity is, it can be taxed as a "C-Corp" which is a taxpayer in its own right separate and apart from its owners; an "S-Corp" which is

---

5 *Alter Ego* claims also apply to any entity and not just to corporations. Another phrase used by lawyers to mean making an *Alter Ego* claim is *"piercing the corporate veil."*

a "pass through entity and taxed similar to a partnership; or as a partnership, which of course is taxed as a partnership. If no election is made, the default for corporations is to be taxed as a "C-Corp," and the default for LLC's and partnerships is to be taxed as a partnership. Importantly, how an entity is taxed has nothing whatsoever to do with whether the owners are personally liable for the debts of the entity. That issue is solely governed by state law.

Downsides of Various Structures

As discussed above the biggest downside of a business structure will always be the imposition of personal liability on the owners. Except with regard to proprietorships and general partnerships where personal liability is built into the structure, most modern business structures will protect their owners from personal liability. As we will discuss in greater detail in Chapter 12, there is always a risk of personal liability to the owners of an otherwise limited liability entity if corporate formalities are not followed.

But there are other bad results which occur when the business becomes insolvent and can't pay its creditors. A simple case study is illustrative. Suppose Aunt Sally and Uncle George form an LLC called "Sally & George's Candy Store, LLC." Unfortunately, the candy store has financial difficulties, and is unable to pay its $100,000 bank loan to Last Good Bank & Trust Company. However, Last Good Bank is willing to compromise the debt and accept $50,000 in full settlement. Aunt Sally and Uncle George are elated, and they take the $50,000 out of their personal savings and pay off Last Good Bank. Without the debt load to the bank, the candy store begins to turn a small profit.

Sound like a good result? It does until early in the following year, when the Candy Store receives an IRS form 1099-C from Last Good Bank showing "cancellation of debt" income ("COD") of $50,000. They have just discovered that cancellation of debt or debt forgiveness results in ordinary income! And adding insult to injury because their business structure is an LLC, and the entity is taxed as a partnership, the cancellation of debt income is passed on to them personally.

The same result would occur in the case of the general partnership, the limited partnership, and the limited liability partnership, assuming that they have elected the default tax procedure. However, if the entity is taxed as a C-Corp or S-Corp, the result is significantly different. In a C-Corp the corporate entity and *not* its shareholders would be liable for the COD income. There is no pass-through to the owners. In an S-Corp although there is a pass-through to the shareholders, *if the corporate entity is insolvent immediately before the cancellation of debt transaction, then there is an exception to the COD income problem for the shareholders in that there will be **no** pass-through of the COD income to the shareholders, to the extent of the insolvency of the S-Corp.* The "insolvency" exclusion is not available to general partnerships, LP's, LLP's or LLC's if they are taxed as partnerships. The exclusion, however, does apply to each of their partners or members if the partner or member is insolvent. In fact you could have a scenario where one partner is insolvent and avoids the COD income, while another is not and has to pay tax on his or her share of the COD income.

These awful cancellation of debt results can also occur when a non-corporate entity like an LLC files bankruptcy. While a discharge (i.e., release of liability) in bankruptcy does not result in cancellation of debt income for the *entity filing bankruptcy*, only that entity gets the exclusion, and unfortunately, the owners still get the pass-through of the COD income.

The "moral of this story" is to consider all possible scenarios when you set up your business structure. Don't just assume that everything throughout the life of the business is going to be rosy. This is especially true if the start-up company is not going to begin with much capital. Get competent accounting and legal advice.

THE LENDER'S BAD DEBT HANDLERS

The Bank Special Assets Department

Years ago, when a borrower defaulted, the banker who made the loan had to deal with and try to collect from the borrower. This created huge problems, and banks learned very expensive lessons about collecting from troubled borrowers. Among the problems was the fact that most line bankers had no idea how to deal with a financially troubled borrower. Secondly, the banker had a self-interest because he or she had made the loan, was responsible for it and likely would suffer professionally if things went wrong. Therefore, the banker could not be objective in handling the work-out. This lack of knowledge and experience coupled with the lack of objectivity resulted in large loan losses, and in some cases, lender liability issues.[6]

Over the years banks got wise to these self-made problems, and they created special departments to handle bad loans. As soon as a loan went into default the handling of the loan was transferred to a work-out specialist

---

6 For reasons which make no sense to me, banks years ago employed young, inexperienced bankers to make and workout million-dollar loans. The banks paid these "kids" very little, and got what they paid for!

in the workout department. The modern name for this department in many banks is the "Special Assets Department."

The Special Assets Department in some banks is run like a separate bank and may be called the "bad bank." It is staffed with supposed trained workout specialists who have no "skin in the game," in that they did not make the loan and are not responsible for it being in trouble. Therefore, they are only rated professionally for how well they perform in the workout of the debt. Thus, if it turns out that the particular loan should not have been made in the first instance and will likely result in a write-off for the bank, that is not a problem for the Special Assets banker as long as he can prove to his supervisor or credit committee that this is the case.

Banks generally do not allow the Special Assets banker to make decisions on his own. Some banks have committees of senior bankers who must pass on the recommendations of the Special Assets banker. I have been in cases where we have made a deal with the Special assets banker only to find that the deal was turned down by the committee. Other banks do not have formal committees, but instead have several senior Special Assets bankers who have approval authority for loans of a certain amount. I have been involved in workouts in which I represented the bank and worked with two individuals who together could approve workout deals for loans of over a billion dollars.

Typically, the Special Assets banker will deal directly with the troubled borrower. When the borrower hires an attorney, the Special Assets banker will bring in the bank's lawyer who could be an in-house lawyer or, more likely, an outside lawyer experienced in litigation and bankruptcy. As I will discuss later in this Book, once lawyers are involved, the workout moves to a higher level, and in many cases, the Special Assets banker will mostly be in the background making decisions, while the lawyers will be in the forefront. The Special Assets banker will generally participate in meetings with the borrower and the borrower's lawyer, but only if his attorney is present.

The Finance Company

Finance Companies have workout departments similar to banks. Like banks the great majority of a finance company's loans are secured loans, and therefore involve the pledge of property as collateral. Depending on what the finance company's collateral is and the structure of the loans, the finance company will have a well-defined department which will handle and monitor the current loans, and it also will have a Special Assets Department charged with collecting defaulted loans and recovering (i.e., repossessing) its collateral.

Accounts receivable financing,[7] where a business borrows money against the pledge of its accounts receivable, requires very specialized monitoring and very specialized workout officers. These people must know how to collect the accounts receivable of a troubled borrower.

The Vendor Creditor

Vendor creditors (e.g., the wholesale seller of inventory or goods to the small business) have a number of different structures for collecting bad debts. Even the smaller vendor will probably have one or more employees in the "credit department." The credit department approves the credit and also deals with customers who default on their accounts. As pointed out above in our discussion of banks, this is not a good structure, and you will find that larger vendors have separated the credit department from the collection department.

---

7 This type of credit facility may involve not just the pledging of accounts receivable as collateral for a term loan, but also an open-ended credit line where the amount of the loan fluctuates with the amount of "eligible" accounts receivable outstanding. That is why it takes special handling by the lender. We will discuss this later in more detail.

The Debt Buyer

In recent years, a new type of creditor has come into the debtor-creditor arena. That is the debt buyer.[8] The debt buyer typically purchases bad debt instruments from banks, credit card issuers and finance companies for cents on the dollar. I will discuss debt buyers later in this Book. Since all of the debts which are purchased by the debt buyer are defaulted loans and bad debt, the debt buyer will generally have a well-defined department which handles the workout and bankruptcy of the borrower. In fact, most of the debt-buyer's organization will be devoted to collecting from the borrower.

Credit Card Companies

This Book in general is written for small businesses not consumers. However, small businesses use credit cards, and that's why I have included this section.

Credit card companies have well defined collection departments which have different levels of activities. When a credit card customer goes into default, the initial collection effort is handled by the company's computer which sends various emails, letters and notices of default and suggests how the customer can cure the default. When that doesn't work, the next level of collector is an individual collector who sits behind a computer and attempts to communicate with the customer. Many of these computer collectors are located in India or other offshore places where staffing this type of activity is cheap.

The collector will try to collect as much information from the customer as he or she can, and at a low level will encourage the customer to pay something on the debt to keep the account from going further in default. Meanwhile, interest at an unconscionable interest rate and late charges

---

8 Debt buyers have been around in bankruptcy cases for many years, but my observation is that the non-bankruptcy debt buyers showed up in mass beginning probably in the1990's.

continue to accumulate, making it likely that the customer will never be able to pay off the debt. The collector at this level may try to get the customer to allow the collector to draft payments out of the customer's bank account. **You should never, never allow this to happen, or to attempt a settlement with the credit card company by allowing it to ACH your checking or savings account.**

Here is a true story of what can happen when a credit card customer allows the credit card company access to his bank account. I represented a gentleman who was suffering from dementia. He came to me along with his wife and daughter. He was having trouble with a credit card company. I normally do not handle consumer cases, but I decided to represent these folks. I contacted the credit card company and began dealing with the level two or three collector. We were close to making a deal for less than 50 cents on the dollar. What I did not know was that the collector was also attempting to contact my client, and he succeeded. Whatever he told my client with dementia will never be known; but he talked him into giving the collector his bank account information. The next day, an electronic ACH withdrawal arrived at my client's bank for the full amount of the debt notwithstanding the fact that the collector and I were negotiating a deal for less than 50 percent.

Thankfully, my client did not have that much money in his account, and the bank refused to honor the ACH. I then contacted the collector, and told him that because of his bad faith, we were no longer going to pay the percentage earlier agreed upon, and now were offering much less. He took the deal! **Remember, the bank is not your friend, and certainly neither is the credit card company.**

Assuming that this level of collector is not getting anywhere with the customer, the next collector is what I call the deal maker. He or she offers to accept 60 cents on the dollar and tells the customer that the credit card company will never agree to anything less. But of course, it will!

After a few more in-house collectors, there may be a period of time when no one contacts the customer. Suddenly there is activity again. This time it is a collection agency or a debt buyer. If you can, it would benefit you to try to determine whether the "representative" you are talking to is employed by a third-party collection agency, the credit card company or whether the credit card company has sold the account to a debt buyer. As we will see later in this Book, who you are dealing with will have a big influence on the type of settlement you can make.

One last comment about credit card collectors: every state has statutes of limitations covering how long a credit card indebtedness is collectible. These can be anywhere from two to six years, depending on the state. You can easily find out what the statute of limitations is in your state by just using *Google*. Depending again on the state, the statute of limitations begins when you default in your payments and continues *so long as you don't make a payment*. During this time and before the expiration of the statute of limitations, the credit card company must file suit against you, or it loses the right to collect the debt. Because most of the collectors are knowledgeable about statutes of limitation, if the statute of limitations has almost expired, many credit card representatives try to get the customer to make a small payment to "show their good faith." **Danger, Danger, Danger!** If you make any payment, no matter how small, it restarts the statute of limitation. You will quickly find out after making the $10 payment, that the credit card collector is not the nice person he was when he talked you into making that payment!

Factors

Factoring is a complicated and misunderstood type of receivables financing, and unfortunately, it is misunderstood by even the small businesses that use it. I will explain how factoring works later in this Book. Suffice it to say that factoring involves the collection of accounts receivable. So, a factor will always have a number of its employees who deal with this type of collection. In larger factors, there is an entire credit department which will approve or disapprove the receivables that are being factored.

Generally, the factoring customer—called the "client"—will deal with one or more employees of the factor who will approve the purchases of the client's receivables. There are also other factor employees who will monitor the accounts, including some who will likely make direct contact with the account debtors from time to time.

There are very few "old line factors" left who actually do factoring in the way it was originally designed. The fees and yield—there is no interest charged—although higher than bank financing, is generally reasonable because these old-line factors take the risk of an account debtor going broke and not paying. It is important to know that most of the current small business factors are disguised "hard money lenders," i.e., they charge exorbitant fees and a disguised "interest," and most are full recourse lenders—meaning if an account doesn't pay, the factoring client is responsible for paying. Using these factors can result in the ruination of a business if the yield is exorbitant.[9]

---

9 Suppose the factor's yield is 25 % on each receivable purchased. What small business can make money on sales or service if 25 % is lopped off the top of its revenues?

A BANKRUPTCY PRIMER

If a troubled borrower cannot work out his, her or its debts, the last resort—and I stress the last resort—is bankruptcy. Most people do not understand how the bankruptcy system works, or even more importantly, when a borrower should consider it.

I have devoted fifty years of my life to bankruptcy law and practice, and I have had the pleasure of teaching bankruptcy law to law students and mentoring some really smart lawyers on bankruptcy law. The following is a short course without too much of the customary legalese on what bankruptcy is and how it works. Later on, in my discussions of how to analyze and resolve financial problems, I will discuss when it is advisable or when it is not advisable to file bankruptcy, and of course which Chapter of the Bankruptcy Code should be considered.

Bankruptcy Law Is Federal Law

Bankruptcy law in the United States is provided for in Article I, Section 8 of the Constitution which gives the Congress the power to among many other things "establish…uniform laws on the subject of bankruptcies throughout the United States." Therefore, bankruptcy law is federal law, and bankruptcy cases are handled by a federal court, not a state court. Importantly, the states have no power or authority to enact bankruptcy laws, and interestingly enough, a change in bankruptcy law may even have retroactive effect.

Congress first enacted bankruptcy laws in this country in response to bad economic times. These laws were usually repealed shortly after the bad times ended, or when the creditor lobby demanded the repeal. The first act was enacted in 1800, and then repealed in 1803. There were other acts in 1837, then 1841, 1867 and then 1898. This latter bankruptcy act has governed bankruptcy in the United States for over a hundred twenty years, although it was substantially amended by the Chandler Act of 1938 and was re-written as the "Bankruptcy Code" in 1978. The Bankruptcy Code is the current bankruptcy law in the United States. Even it has been amended a number of times.

The last major amendments occurred in 2005 in a federal law known as the Bankruptcy Abuse Prevention and Consumer Protection Act ("BAPCPA"). They were enacted in response to lobbying[10] by the credit card industry. The credit card industry believed that it was being unfairly treated in consumer bankruptcy cases because debtors were able to dis-charge credit card debt without paying back the indebtedness they owed. The credit card industry was successful and convinced Congress to enact the 2005 amendments. The 2005 amendments were largely written by law-yers with little bankruptcy experience while the original Bankruptcy Code was written by bankruptcy law scholars, Bankruptcy Judges and practi-tioners. In my opinion, the 2005 amendments neither prevented abuse nor protected consumers, were unnecessary, and in fact made it tougher on consumers and small businesses. Not only did the Amendments not pro-vide more debt payments for the credit card industry, but many sections of the Amendments were written in such a way as to not make practical sense.

---

10 A powerful congressman who was chair of the House Judiciary Committee told me many years ago that the banks and other creditors had plenty of lobbyists, but there were **no** lobbyists in the House and Senate who represented the interests of debtors. That is true not only in Congress, but also in the state legislatures.

Debtors and Creditors

There are several parties in a typical bankruptcy case. There is the "**Debtor**"[11] who is the person or entity which **owes** the money to the "**Creditor**" which is the bank, finance company or vendor who is **owed** the money and is extending the credit. There is one debtor,[12] but possibly numerous creditors. Most of the creditors are unsecured, that is, they do not hold any collateral. Usually, there are one or more creditors who hold security interests[13] in the assets of the debtor. A "**Bankruptcy Judge**" decides the factual and legal disputes in the bankruptcy case and confirms (i.e., approves) plans proposed under Chapters 11, 12 and 13, as discussed below. The Bankruptcy Judge is a federal judicial officer appointed for a fourteen-year term by the United States Circuit Court for the area of the country where the Bankruptcy Judge serves. The Bankruptcy Court in which the Bankruptcy Judge presides is part of the United States District Court, which is the trial court in the federal judiciary system.

Another party in bankruptcy cases is the Trustee who is automatically appointed in Chapters 7, 12 and 13. The trustee can be appointed in a regular Chapter 11 case[14] and is appointed in small business cases under what is called "Sub-chapter V." As discussed further below, the Chapter 7 trustee liquidates the debtor's non-exempt assets and makes distributions to creditors. The Chapter 12 and the Chapter 13 trustees are usually "standing trustees" who serve in all of the Chapter 12 and Chapter 13 cases in their particular district. Their function in each case is to evaluate the particular case, serve as disbursing agent for payments which the trustee collects from the debtor and to make distributions to creditors in accordance with the Chapter 12 or Chapter 13 plan. In Sub-Chapter V, the Trustee acts

---

11 Under the bankruptcy act of 1898, the Debtor was called the "Bankrupt;" but that term is no longer used or defined in the Bankruptcy Code.

12 The Code does allow for a husband and wife to file a joint bankruptcy. So, in that case, there would be two debtors.

13 Secured lending is discussed in Chapter 4 of this book.

14 Chapter 11 of this book is devoted entirely to discussing Chapter 11.

as a mediator and tries to help the debtor and creditors come up with a consensus plan.

In 1978 Congress established a governmental entity called the United States Trustee Program which is part of the United States Justice Department. The program was created because of lobbying efforts by the bank and vendor creditors which claimed that many bankruptcy cases involved fraudulent behavior by debtors and trustees.[15] It initially was a pilot program in 18 federal districts and then expanded to all of the states other than Alabama and North Carolina in 1986. It is responsible for overseeing the administration of bankruptcy cases and supervising private trustees in bankruptcy in all of the states other than Alabama and North Carolina.[16] There are representatives of the U.S. Trustee Program in each of the federal districts covered by the Program. A representative of the U.S. Trustee is assigned to every bankruptcy case and is a "party in interest" in every case. That means that they can appear and argue in favor or against any issue which is being presented to the Bankruptcy Judge. The U.S. Trustee also appoints trustees and creditors' committees in Chapter 11 cases and monitors the trustees and their activities.

Chapter What?

The bankruptcy code is divided into chapters and sections. Chapters 1, 3, 5, 7, 11, 12 and 13 are the relevant ones for individuals and small businesses. There are five different kinds of bankruptcy proceedings: Chapter 7, Chapter 11, Chapter 12 and Chapter 13 plus Chapter 9 which is for governmental entities and is not discussed in this Book. Chapter 7 and Chapter 13 are mostly for consumers, although Chapter 7 can be used by any person

---

15 I have always believed that while there was some fraud, it was not widespread, and it was generally dealt with by the authorities.

16 Powerful senators in Alabama and North Carolina insisted that the U.S. Trustee Program not be installed in their states. In those states the U.S. Trustee role is filled by Bankruptcy Administrators who are not part of the Justice Department but are appointed by the U.S. Circuit Court of Appeals covering those states and therefore are part of the federal judiciary.

or entity who is not prohibited by the Bankruptcy Code from filing a bankruptcy such as an insurance company or bank, and Chapter 13 can be used by a small business proprietorship. Chapter 12 can be used only by family farmers and family fishermen.

The Supreme Court has also promulgated "Bankruptcy Rules" which govern Bankruptcy Court procedure. Importantly, the Bankruptcy Rules have the force of law and must be followed by debtors and creditors.

Chapter 7 involves a liquidation of a Debtor's assets. The liquidation is managed by a Trustee appointed by the United States Trustee or elected by the creditors. The debtor initiates[17] the bankruptcy case by filing a petition and also schedules of assets and liabilities, income and a statement of financial affairs. If the Debtor is an individual, the Debtor is entitled to exempt certain property of a certain value and even in some instances cash. Although the Bankruptcy Code contains an entire section on what these exemptions can be, there is also a provision permitting any state to opt out of the federal exemption and apply its own. Most states have opted out, and what is left, depending on the state where the bankruptcy is filed, are very liberal exemptions or very restricted exemptions. The debtor is also entitled in some instances to remove a judgment lien which encumbers his or her exempt property.

The basic concept of Chapter 7 in the case of an individual Debtor as opposed to an entity such as a corporation or an LLC is that the individual Debtor turns over all of his or her non-exempt assets to the Trustee. The Trustee then liquidates the assets (i.e., turns them into cash by sale or auction) and then pays out the money to the creditors in accordance with the priorities established by the Bankruptcy Code. These priorities require that domestic support obligations,[18] administrative expenses of the bankruptcy, wages, taxes and several other debts be paid first, while unsecured general creditors get paid last out of the liquidation proceeds.

---

17 There is a provision in the Bankruptcy Code for creditors to file an involuntary bankruptcy against a Debtor.

18 These are essentially alimony, maintenance and support obligations.

If the Debtor is an honest debtor, he or she will receive a discharge which is a release of all of his or her liabilities to creditors. If the debtor has violated any of a "laundry list" of dishonest acts, he or she will **not** receive a discharge of that particular debt.[19] Egregious conduct like fraudulently transferring property within one year before filing bankruptcy in order to defraud creditors will result, if proven, in a debtor not receiving a discharge of any of his or her debts. Thankfully, the bankruptcy law *favors* the granting of a discharge, and there is a heavy burden on creditors to prove that a debt is non-dischargeable.

In a Chapter 7 there are some debts like certain types of domestic support obligations and recent taxes for which the debtor will not receive a discharge in any event. In most Chapter 7 consumer cases the debtor does in fact get a discharge of his or her debts. Since Chapter 7 is a liquidation chapter, the Bankruptcy Code does not permit an entity such as a corporation or LLC to get a discharge or release of its debts. Thus, the entity is liquidated in bankruptcy, but receives no discharge of its debts. In fact, this same principal applies even in Chapter 11 and Chapter 12 if the entity is being liquidated as opposed to being reorganized.

Chapter 13 is what used to be called a "wage earner" proceeding, but as I said above is now available to small proprietorships. There are debt limits which restrict those who are eligible to file a Chapter 13.[20] In a Chapter 13 a Debtor files a plan which must be approved by the Court, and which proposes to pay the Debtor's creditors over time. The plan may pay 100 % of the claims of creditors or result in payment of less than 100 % to some creditors. A "standing trustee" monitors the case and may handle the payments made under the plan. The installment pay out may last from three to five years.

---

19 The "laundry list" includes giving a false financial statement, causing malicious injury to the property of another and defrauding another person.

20 The debt limits in a Chapter 13 and dollar limits in other provisions of the Bankruptcy Code may go up as the consumer Price Index rises. Of course, Congress may change the dollar figures whenever it wants.

Chapter 13 cases these days are either filed to enable a consumer debtor (or small proprietorship) to keep an asset such as his or her house or car which has equity in it over and above the mortgage or security interest; or they are filed simply as an alternative to Chapter 7. In the equity situation, the Chapter 13 debtor would keep the assets and continue to pay the mortgage holders on the house and car. After paying his or her lawyer and other bankruptcy related expenses, the debtor would pay the balance of the equity to unsecured creditors over three to five years. If there is little or no equity in the debtor's assets, the Chapter 13 debtor continues to pay the secured debt on the house and car and pays little or nothing to the unsecured creditors.

On the other hand, if a Chapter 7 were filed instead of a Chapter 13, the Trustee would sell the assets to realize the equity, pay off the mortgages and distribute the equity to unsecured creditors. In the case where there is little or no equity in the debtor's assets, the result for the unsecured creditors in a Chapter 13 would be very similar to what would happen in a Chapter 7.

There appear to be differing statistics, but I believe that a significant number of Chapter 13 cases are just "pipe dreams," and are not successful.[21]

Chapter 11 is available to individuals and all types of business organizations. It essentially involves a reorganization or liquidation of the "debtor" in what can be an expensive, lengthy and complicated process–except in the case of a small business filing which is known as Sub-Chapter V. Once a Chapter 11 case is filed, the debtor is called the "Debtor in Possession" because, unlike in a Chapter 7 case, the debtor *remains in possession of its assets and business operations*. Chapter 11 is an important remedy for a small business, and therefore I have devoted an entire Chapter of this Book to it.

---

21 I don't like criticizing my fellow bankruptcy lawyers who practice in the consumer area, but my observation has been that many Chapter 13's are filed for the benefit of the lawyer because if the Chapter 13 lasts for a few months, the lawyer will receive his or her fees either in full, or at least collect a substantial amount of the fees. It thus permits the lawyer to file the Chapter 13 without requiring much or anything in the nature of a fee retainer—which is a real marketing tool. Unfortunately, in many of these filings what the debtor needed was a Chapter 7 and not a Chapter 13.

Chapter 12 is a reorganization or liquidation proceeding for farmers and fishermen only. Debtors with debts up to $10 million may qualify for filing a Chapter 12 case. Like Sub-Chapter V[22], it is a stream-lined proceeding with the aim of making it easier and cheaper for farmers and fishermen to get the benefit of bankruptcy. Just as in Sub-Chapter V, a trustee is appointed who has oversight and monitoring duties, but the Debtor continues to be in possession of the Debtor's assets and to conduct its farming business. The Debtor files a plan proposing a payment structure to creditors, which is confirmed by the Court if it complies with various requirements of the Bankruptcy Code.

Filing the Petition in Consumer Cases: On Your Own or Through an Attorney

It is possible for individuals to file their own bankruptcies. These individuals are called *pro se*[23] debtors. However, in most states a non-lawyer cannot file a bankruptcy for an *entity* like an LLC or a corporation. The reason for this is that most state laws prohibit a non-lawyer from representing an entity even if the non-lawyer is the owner. Even if a non-lawyer principal is permitted to represent the entity in Chapter 7, it is unwise.

Regarding consumer cases it is fairly commonplace now to see *pro se* debtors—that is, debtors who do not employ lawyers—filing Chapter 7 or Chapter 13 cases on their own. The obvious "benefit" to the consumer *pro se* debtor is that they don't have to pay fees to a lawyer. In many cases the *pro se* debtors find the bankruptcy forms online. Sometimes a *pro se* debtor will hire a paralegal or other person who holds themselves out as being skilled in preparing the necessary paperwork for a bankruptcy filing but are not lawyers. These "bankruptcy petition preparers" usually charge a fee for their "services."

---

22 See Chapter 11 of this Book for a discussion of this bankruptcy remedy.

23 *Pro se* is a Latin phrase which literally means "for oneself." In the context of filing a bankruptcy or participating in litigation, it means representing yourself in court.

Section 110 of the Bankruptcy Code governs "bankruptcy petition preparers." Bankruptcy petition preparers are forbidden by law to give legal advice, and they cannot represent the debtor during the bankruptcy case. Since neither the bankruptcy petition preparer nor the *pro se* debtor is a lawyer, how does the *pro se* debtor know whether he even should file a bankruptcy? Thus, how can the *pro se* debtor determine before filing whether he will end up losing all of his or her assets, and perhaps not even get a discharge because of some wrongful act he or she has committed prior to bankruptcy? Finally, what if the *pro se* debtor made a fraudulent transfer of some asset like his or her home to a spouse prior to bankruptcy? The trustee in bankruptcy is most surely going to sue the spouse to recover the transfer, and if the transfer occurred within a year before filing the bankruptcy with the intent to defraud creditors, the *pro se* debtor is not going to get a discharge of his or her debts.

In seminars where I have spoken, I have likened the *pro se* debtor to a sick patient who has determined without medical help that he or she needs an appendectomy and is attempting to operate on himself or herself. While my observation is that Bankruptcy Judges do everything they can to help the *pro se* debtor through the bankruptcy proceeding, there is a limit to what a judge can do. There are numerous lawyers who specialize in representing debtors in a consumer bankruptcy case—Chapter 7 or Chapter 13. The fees they charge may differ dramatically; and unfortunately, the quality of the advice the consumer debtor receives may also differ.

My advice to you if you think you need to file a bankruptcy is to follow the suggestions below:

- Contact a reputable bankruptcy lawyer, perhaps someone recommended by a friend or associate who has had a good experience.

- Tell the lawyer everything you can about your financial situation and be truthful. Bankruptcy is federal law and lying on bankruptcy papers is a federal crime.

- Bring documents with you like collection notices, copies of mortgages and other debt instruments, tax returns and a copy of any lawsuit which may have been filed against you.

- Do your homework before you have your consultation—read about bankruptcy, and especially about what debts are not dischargeable.

- Insist on speaking with the licensed lawyer—do not settle for a consultation with a paralegal or other office personnel. If the licensed lawyer can't see you, go somewhere else.

- At the consultation, ask plenty of questions, and make sure you discuss the lawyer's fees and how the fees will be paid.

Finally, if you don't get along or don't like the lawyer or for whatever reason don't trust his or her advice, **do not employ the lawyer**. There are plenty of other bankruptcy lawyers.

Multiple Filings

Some people attempt to "game" every situation they can. In other words, they try to manipulate the system, sometimes unlawfully, to their advantage. Institutions like the judicial system simply do not have enough safeguards or protections to prevent this type of misconduct, and they never will. I was once involved in a case, where the *pro se* debtor appealed every order of the Bankruptcy Judge all the way to the U.S. Supreme Court. In each instance, although the appeal was frivolous, each appeal required an appellate court to go through the normal procedures of deciding the appeal and writing an order. All of this took judicial time and effort. To make matters worse, this particular debtor also sued as many judges as he could along the way.

These debtors have figured out a way to stop foreclosures and repossessions by filing multiple *pro se* bankruptcies. As will be discussed in the next section of this Chapter, when a bankruptcy petition is filed, the Automatic Stay stops all creditor action against the debtor and the debtor's property. Therefore, when a debtor files a bankruptcy petition, the foreclosure or repossessions are immediately stopped. Once the case is filed, the multiple filing debtor doesn't follow the Court's orders or doesn't respond to the trustee, causing the case to get dismissed. The multiple filer may wait until the creditor asks for relief from the automatic stay and then files a motion to dismiss the case. As each one gets dismissed, the debtor waits until the last minute before the foreclosure and files another one. Congress has attempted to remedy this unlawful conduct by modifying the application of the Automatic Stay (discussed below) in the event of multiple filings.

The Automatic Stay

One of the reasons the bankruptcy system works for debtors and creditors is because it created a very specialized court in which the disputes between the debtor and the debtor's creditors can be resolved in a fair and equitable way. In most situations involving a financially troubled debtor, there are one or more—or many—debt collection proceedings or foreclosures pending at the time the bankruptcy is filed. If the bankruptcy is to work properly, all of these collection proceedings must be stopped when the bankruptcy proceeding is initiated, and the validity, priority and extent of the claims of these creditors or parties must be determined by the Bankruptcy Court rather than by the state or federal court in which the disputes were being litigated.

Section 362 of the Bankruptcy Code provides for an **Automatic Stay** to go into effect upon the filing of the Debtor's Petition. In the prior Bankruptcy Act, which was replaced by the Bankruptcy Code, the court would enter an injunction upon the filing of the bankruptcy case. The injunction would restrain creditors from taking any action, with some exceptions, against the debtor or the debtor's property. In 1973 when the first Bankruptcy Rules went into effect, the Rules replaced the injunction with an automatic stay which had the same effect—prohibiting collection actions against debtors and their assets.

The legislative history makes it clear that Congress intended that the Automatic Stay be pervasive. The evolving case law also makes it clear that there are very serious consequences for anyone violating the Automatic Stay.

The concept of the Automatic Stay is relatively simple and logical. First, with a few exceptions it prevents any action, or the continuation of any action against the debtor to enforce any judgment or claim. The exceptions generally involve the enforcement of federal and state police actions and the continuation of criminal contempt proceedings.

Second, in Chapters 7 and 11, the Automatic Stay precludes any action against the property of the debtor in existence at the time of the filing of the bankruptcy. This is the property of the debtor which becomes and forms the "property of the bankruptcy estate", and which is turned over to the Trustee at the time of filing in a Chapter 7 or is administered by the Debtor in Possession or a Trustee in a Chapter 11. In a Chapter 11 property that is acquired after the filing—for example, inventory purchased, and revenues received—also become part of the bankruptcy estate and subject to the automatic stay.

In Chapters 12 and 13, the Automatic Stay also precludes any action against property acquired after the filing of the bankruptcy so long as the case is pending. Finally, since the enactment of the 2005 amendments, which is discussed above, the post-petition income of an individual debtor (e.g., income earned after the filing) in Chapter 11 is also included in the property of the estate and therefore subject to protection by the Automatic Stay.

In sum, the Automatic Stay stops personal actions against a bankruptcy debtor like lawsuits and other collection activities, and also stops actions which would have the effect of encumbering, taking possession of, or foreclosing property of the debtor and property of the bankruptcy estate.

The Automatic Stay continues in effect with regard to property of the Estate until the earlier of the time when the particular property is no longer property of the estate, e.g., it is sold or abandoned, and the time the case is closed. The Automatic Stay continues as to actions against the debtor until the debtor receives or is denied a discharge. If the debtor is granted a discharge, then the Automatic Stay ends, but is replaced by a Discharge Injunction which restrains actions against the debtor to enforce a discharged debt.

Filing a Chapter 7 for a Corporation or Other Entity

Filing a Chapter 7 for a corporation, limited liability company or other entity is hardly ever advisable. For one thing an entity does not receive a discharge after it is liquidated in Chapter 7. So, if there is some reason the owners want to use the entity again after bankruptcy, it will still owe the balance of its debts which were not paid in the bankruptcy.[24]

Another reason for not filing a Chapter 7 for an entity is what I call the "Halloween Risk." By that I mean that it is common for closely held companies to have "skeletons in their closet." For example, the company has been paying the personal debts of the owners or obligations of another affiliated company owned by the same people; or it has been repaying "loans" made by its owners.[25] These are just three examples of skeletons. You can be sure that the trustee in bankruptcy will be investigating and looking into all of these skeletons, and he or she may well institute suit against the owners or others to recover such sums.

Thus, the better remedy is to let the entity just die—out of court! That said, there are a few instances—not many—in which a Chapter 7

---

24 I can't think of any reason why an owner would want to re-use the corporate entity of an entity which has been liquidated in Chapter 7. Similarly, there is no reason to re-use an entity that has been liquidated out of court or goes out of business owing debts.

25 There are numerous cases decided against the owners of companies with little or no capital where the owners *loaned* money to the company rather than providing equity infusions.

bankruptcy might be advisable. For example, suppose a company owes a substantial amount of payroll taxes and unsecured vendor debts. The principals are going to be personally liable for the trust fund part of the taxes. They may not be liable for the vendor debt. If the company has unencumbered assets or it has equity over and above its secured debt, it might be a good idea to consider filing a Chapter 7 for it because the tax debt will have *priority* under the Bankruptcy Code over and above the unsecured vendor debt. That means that any money obtained by the trustee through liquidation of the assets of the company, after payment of administrative expenses, will be paid first to priority creditors like the taxing authorities. Thus, if the vendor creditors are suing the company and perhaps near obtaining judgments, it may be a good idea to stop the "creditor grab" and let a Trustee liquidate the company.

Another scenario in which a Chapter 7 might be the correct debtor's relief remedy for an entity would be where the bank has a security interest in all or most of the assets of the company. Your good friend, the bank, has turned out not to be your friend and is foreclosing, and you have guaranteed the debt. It turns out that there is substantial equity in the bank's collateral over and above what is owed the bank. If the collateral is liquidated in an orderly process, there will not only be enough money to pay the bank in full, but enough money to pay taxes and even some money to pay the unsecured creditors. A Chapter 7 or Chapter 11 might be warranted in this case. Employ a competent commercial lawyer to represent and advise you.

Preferences

The Trustee or Debtor in Possession also has certain powers set forth in the Bankruptcy Code which permit the Trustee or Debtor in Possession to recover monies which were paid by the debtor prior to bankruptcy to its creditors. These "preferential transfers" are payments or other transfers of value which were made out of the ordinary course of business or out of ordinary business terms on an existing unsecured indebtedness within ninety days[26] of the filing of the bankruptcy when the debtor was insolvent.[27] When the trustee or debtor in possession sues the creditor to recover a preference, it is said that the trustee or debtor in possession is suing to "avoid" the preference.

Preference avoidance has been in our law for many years. Congress put the preference section in the Bankruptcy Code in order to "even the playing field" for creditors, some of whom are more aggressive than others in collecting debts or have more information about the debtor than others. Of all of the provisions of the Bankruptcy Code, the provisions which probably anger creditors the most are the provisions for avoidance of preferences!

Here's an example of a preference which is avoidable by a Trustee. Little Business, LLC is insolvent (assets less than liabilities) and is being hounded by the collection agency for one of its vendors, Big Supplier, Inc. Little Business, LLC owes Big Supplier, Inc. $100,000.00 and also owes lots of other creditors; but the other creditors are not as aggressive as Big Supplier, Inc. Little Business, LLC finally relents and sends $10,000.00 to the collection agency for the benefit of Big Supplier, Inc. Within ninety days after the payment, Little Business, LLC files a Chapter 7 bankruptcy. Under this factual scenario, the trustee of Little Business, LLC can sue Big Supplier, Inc. in the Bankruptcy Court and recover the $10,000.00 for the benefit of all creditors. In other words, the $10,000.00 will go back into the bankruptcy estate "pot" to be distributed to all of the creditors, including Big Supplier, Inc., who now will have an additional unsecured claim equal to the $10,000.00 it had to pay the Trustee. Put another way, Big Supplier,

---

26 If the payment or other transfer was made to what is called an *insider*, then the time period for avoidance is one year. Insiders include relatives, affiliates and similar persons or entities.

27 Insolvency is a big deal in bankruptcy cases, and there is a presumption during the 90 days prior to the bankruptcy filing that the debtor *is* insolvent. There are two types of insolvency: equitable and legal. Equitable insolvency is the inability to pay one's debts as they come due. Legal insolvency occurs when the debtor's assets are less than the debtor's liabilities. Preferences only occur where there is legal insolvency. However, in avoidance actions in the bankruptcy court and under the Uniform Voidable Transactions Act, equitable insolvency may create a presumption of legal insolvency which has to be rebutted by the party sued by the Trustee or Debtor in Possession. Finally, equitable insolvency is one of the grounds for filing an involuntary bankruptcy.

Inc. is now back where it was before it extracted the $10,000.00 payment from Little Business, LLC—it is still owed $100,000.00. This is, of course, what galls creditors the most about the preference law!

It is important to note that there are a number of defenses a creditor has against a Trustee's attempt to avoid a preference. Among these are that the payment was made in the ordinary course of business or according to ordinary business terms or that it was meant as a *contemporaneous exchange*—in other words, the parties did not intend for the transaction to be a credit transaction, and it wasn't. Another defense is called the *subsequent advance* exception. It provides protection to the creditor who receives a preference, but after receiving the preference extends further unsecured credit.

I have watched the law change in the preference area over the many years I have practiced in the bankruptcy and commercial law areas. It is very interesting to me how the big-creditor lobby has from time to time over the years tried to get Congress to water-down the preference law—and they have been generally successful as you can expect. Of course, making exceptions to the preference law hurts smaller creditors because whatever money the trustee collects by avoiding a preference goes into the "pot" for ultimate payment to all of the unsecured creditors. So, while the big creditors won't have to pay back what would have been a preference, the small creditors are prevented from sharing in that payment. Just as in the case of small business debtors, there is little or no effective lobby in Congress for the many "Mom and Pop" small business creditors. After all, many of the small businesses for which I wrote this Book are also the Mom and Pop creditors of other small businesses.

Fraudulent or Voidable Transfers

Finally, the Bankruptcy Code permits the Trustee or Debtor in Possession to "avoid" fraudulent or "voidable" transfers of property. These transfers occur many times as some sort of "asset protection" scheme which is employed by the debtor to keep his or her assets from being taken by creditors. This type of litigation is becoming more and more common, and it sometimes is initiated by creditors before bankruptcy. When the debtor files for bankruptcy, the litigation becomes property of the bankruptcy estate and is taken over by the trustee or debtor in possession. The case may be transferred (called, "removed") to the Bankruptcy Court from another court, or it may continue in the other court.

Because of the relationship between fraudulent or voidable transfers and asset protection, I have included a discussion of both in Chapter 7 of this Book.

CHAPTER 4

SECURED LENDING

In modern times, bank and finance company loans to individuals and small businesses are almost always secured. There is little or no unsecured lending by institutional lenders, and unsecured lending really exists only for vendor open account debt which I will discuss below. Occasionally I have seen some "hard-money lenders"[28] make unsecured loans, but the interest rates charged are near or actually usurious.[29]

Where secured loans are secured by business assets, the loans are said to be "asset-based" secured loans. In making these loans, the lender is relying on the strength of the borrower's assets. In the underwriting of the loan, the lender will place values on the collateral, and the loan amount is directly proportionate to the amount of these values. In "open ended" asset-based loans, the amount of the loan fluctuates depending on how much the values of the assets are at any particular time.

---

28 "Hard Money Lenders" used to be mobsters, but now the phrase is used to include all lenders who typically charge exorbitant fees and interest—not always usurious—and generally only lend to businesses that already have cash flow or even financial problems. I discuss hard money lenders later in this Chapter.

29 All states have statutes which govern how much interest can be charged on a loan. Unfortunately, some of the rate caps have exceptions which may include small loans, or loans made pursuant to a written contract which may have much larger cap. Banks and other institutions may be exempt. In my home state of Georgia any rate over 5 % per month (60 % per year) is usurious, but the penalty is only the forfeiture of the interest and possible misdemeanor criminal conviction.

"Personal Property" Collateral

Secured lending is governed by Article 9 of the Uniform Commercial Code (called the "UCC") if the collateral consists of personal property.[30] It means that the borrower has pledged some personal property to the bank or finance company to secure the loan. The legal jargon is that the lender has taken a "security interest" in the personal property which is then called the lender's "collateral."

In a garden variety secured business loan, the bank or finance company will take a security interest in the borrower's accounts receivable, inventory and/or equipment and perhaps a mortgage on real estate owned by the debtor or some other person. The security interest in the accounts receivable, inventory and equipment is usually in the property that is existing at the time the loan is made plus future personal property (called, "after acquired" accounts receivable, inventory, etc.). Thus, the bank's collateral will consist of the accounts and/or inventory existing on the date the loan is made plus all new accounts receivable, and all new inventory purchased afterwards. If the collateral also consists of equipment, then the bank will have a security interest in all newly purchased equipment.

Real Estate Collateral

Real estate collateral is not ordinarily governed by the UCC but is covered by separate state law. There is no uniform law governing how real estate is handled—each state has its own separate law. That means that the instruments used to grant a security interest in real estate are different in each state. These instruments may be called mortgages, deeds of trust, security deeds or other names given to the instrument by state law. How these instruments are signed, filed of record and the priority these instruments have over other like instruments or liens is also governed by each state's law.

---

30 "Personal Property" is defined as all property other than real property.

Documentation of the Secured Loan

The documentation of a garden variety secured loan will usually consist of four main agreements plus special "perfection" documents which the lender will file to perfect its security interest or mortgage on the borrower's property. The first will be the "credit agreement" which summarizes the loan terms and will likely contain covenants, warranties and events of default discussed below. The second document will be the "promissory note" or "note" which is the borrower's promise to pay the debt. The third agreement will be the "security agreement" in which the borrower pledges the personal property collateral to the lender. Finally, and last, but certainly not least will be the personal guarantee or guarantees. These are also discussed in Chapter 5.

If there is personal property collateral, there will be another document called a "financing statement" (also called a UCC-1) which used to be signed by the borrower. Now the signature of the borrower is no longer required, and the UCC-1 is completed and filed of record by the lender. The UCC-1 will give the name and contact information for the lender and the borrower and, among other things, will describe the collateral. The UCC statute in each state will provide for where the UCC-1 is filed.[31]

The UCC-1, when properly completed and filed is notice to the world of the existence of a security interest in the property of the borrower. It protects the lender from a later security interest or lien obtained by another creditor of the borrower on the same property. The legal jargon is that it "perfects" the lender's security interest. On the other hand, if it is not filed correctly or doesn't adequately describe the collateral, then the security interest of the lender will not be perfected. Importantly, the failure to properly perfect the security interest only affects the relationship between the lender and any other creditors of the borrower who claim a security

---

31 Depending on what state you live in, the UCC-1 may be filed with a clerk of court, the office of the secretary of state or some other governmental officer.

interest or lien. It does not invalidate the security interest as between the lender and the borrower.

Finally, if there is real estate collateral, there will be one or more other documents which will be whatever instruments are required by state law to create and perfect the lender's security interest in the real estate collateral, e.g., mortgage, deed of trust, etc.

The larger the loan and the more complicated the collateral securing it, the more documents are required. For example, a lender may want to take a security interest in a stock account, bank account or insurance policy of the borrower or guarantor. This type of collateral requires specialized documentation which creates the security interest and perfects it.

Covenants and Warranties

Most of the credit agreements involving security interests in the borrower's assets have a number of what are called "covenants." These are a list of "boilerplate" promises and, depending on the amount and complexity of the loan, certain additional covenants tailored to the particular borrower's business and financial situation. For example, a typical covenant would be a promise by the borrower not to use the proceeds of the loan for anything but operation of the business in the normal course. Another might be to keep the collateral insured and protected. You get the idea. You should always read the covenants for at least two reasons. First, regarding the "boilerplate" form promises, these covenants might not really be appropriate to the type of business you are operating or loan you are obtaining. Thus, if you intend some of the proceeds of the loan to fund a subsidiary company, that might be a breach of a covenant to only use the loan proceeds for operating the primary business. Secondly, in the event you or the company goes bankrupt, a breach of these covenants could cause problems with an individual's discharge or in making a reorganization in a Chapter 11 work.

All credit agreements also contain "warranties." These are a list of promises by the borrower that certain things about the borrower are true. For example, a credit agreement may contain a warranty that the person signing the loan agreements has the corporate authority to do so or that the borrower is registered with the corporate authorities of the state and is in good standing. They always include "boilerplate" warranties, but just as in the case of covenants, these boilerplate warranties can be inapplicable to the particular borrower. You need to read through all of them.

Some of the more important warranties are that the company is current on its taxes (payroll and income), is solvent and does not have a present intention of filing bankruptcy. I have always thought that the solvency warranty is really a trap for a small business. Most small businesses, even though hopefully profitable, don't either have or keep a lot of capital. Excess funds are paid to the owners in the form of distributions or salaries. Capital purchases (called "CAPEX" in accounting jargon) are usually made through loans. So, for example, a small business which is adequately capitalized might "write a check" for the purchase of a new machine or truck. A small business which has limited capital will simply apply for a loan from the bank or finance company in order to make a CAPEX purchase. However, the thinly capitalized small business may be a real money-maker and have no financial problems whatsoever.

But the solvency warranty is even more of a trap for the small business because as discussed in the previous chapter, it has two definitions: legal insolvency—assets less than liabilities; and equitable insolvency—the business is not paying its debts as they come due. I usually counsel potential borrowers to but an asterisk by the solvency warranty and say that the warranty only is that the business is current with all of its creditors, or like language.[32]

As with breaches of covenants, the breaches of warranties can also result in problems in a later individual bankruptcy or business bankruptcy.

---

32 In later chapters I will repeat the two different kinds of insolvency because they are very important to different types of issues, including bankruptcy issues.

For example, in a business loan agreement, a standard warranty provision states that the borrower is current on all of its taxes. Suppose you sign the agreement, but really aren't current on perhaps the company's payroll taxes. The company then goes into default with the lender and fails. This breach of warranty might be enough to result in your guaranteed debt becoming non-dischargeable in *your* bankruptcy.[33] We will cover more on covenants and warranties in Chapter 10 on workouts.

Online Hard Money Lenders

In recent years, a new "cottage" billion-dollar lending industry has arisen. These lenders appear to be the friends of small businesses, and their TV commercials show testimonials of happy customers. These lenders are really disguised hard-money lenders. Interest rates or yields are exorbitant and can be higher than 30 % APR. In some instances, it is really difficult to determine what the true interest rate is because there are so many fees and costs which are built into the loan. Most of these loans are done online and are so streamlined that part of their attractiveness is how easy the application process is. Buried in the small online print is the personal guarantee of all of the principals. Moreover, most of my clients who have borrowed from hard-money lenders do not realize that they also are pledging *all* of the business' assets as collateral. It's in the fine print! And that becomes problematical when the business already has a secured loan like an SBA loan where the lender has taken a security interest in all or some of the assets of the business. The hard money lender then has a second priority security interest in the business' assets which may make it difficult, for example, to refinance the first loan or even to sell the assets of the business without paying off the hard money lender.

Here is a dose of reality. Do you know any business that can make money or even break even paying 25 % or 30% interest on a line of credit? I don't!

---

33 Under the Bankruptcy Code, the breach of warranty could be construed as a false financial statement.

Small Business Factors

Small business factoring has grown by leaps and bounds over the last twenty-five years or so. They have taken the place of what was known as "old-line" factors. Generally, the cost of old-line factoring is somewhat higher than bank financing, but there are advantages to old-line factoring. For example, when these factors purchase an account receivable owed by an account debtor whose credit they have approved, if the account debtor defaults, the old-line factor absorbs the loss, not the factoring client.

Most of the newer factors are **full recourse** factors, meaning that they "buy" an account receivable, but if the account debtor (i.e., customer of the borrower-factoring client) doesn't pay in an agreed upon time (e.g., 90 days), then the amount advanced is charged back to the borrower-factoring client). The courts have long held that this type of factoring is a disguised secured lending arrangement, and that rather than actually purchasing an account receivable, the "factor" is in reality only lending against the receivable.[34] Some of the newer factors also charge exorbitant fees and interest. In reality these factors are hard-money lenders. And of course, you can expect that the factor is going to want a personal guarantee!

The factoring agreement contains a lot of surprises for the unsuspecting borrower (still called a "client" even though the arrangement is a disguised secured lending arrangement). For example, there are various fees charged during the arrangement; there is a reserve equal to a certain percentage of each receivable factored which is held by the factor and usually released only to the client when the factor feels like it; and of course, as I have said previously, there is full recourse on any account which goes beyond the aging date that is agreed upon in the factoring agreement.

---

34 Those of us who practice in the commercial area generally understand factoring. The majority of customers and probably general practice lawyers unfortunately do not understand factoring. I have tried cases in which the only persons at the trial who understood factoring were the witness who was an employee of the factor and me. How to explain factoring to a jury and a judge who was a former prosecutor is quite a challenge!

Most factors never like to use the term "interest" in discussing what they charge their clients. This is the mystique of factoring. Whether what they charge is called discount rates, interest, fees, commissions or whatever, it is imperative that the prospective client understand how these charges compare with bank financing. My advice is that any small business considering entering into a full recourse factoring agreement should think twice and avoid this type of lending, especially if the fees charged by the factor are exorbitant. As a small businessperson, it is imperative that you know how much your business can afford to pay a lender for the use of its money. Just as importantly, you need to know whether your credit customers are good enough risks for factoring. If they are not, factoring is going to end up as a disastrous choice.[35]

At the very least, employ an attorney who has experience in dealing with factoring to help you understand and negotiate the terms. Remember that factoring is a very specialized kind of lending, and only commercial attorneys with experience is this type of lending can advise you properly.

Vendor Debt

Most small businesses have open account debt. These vendors sell goods and services on credit. Many times, this kind of debt is just unsecured debt, i.e., the vendor does not take a security interest in any of the property of the business. Other vendors, especially vendors who are selling equipment on credit, will require the business to grant a security interest in the equipment or goods sold.[36] Finally, as I discuss in the next chapter regarding vendor personal guarantees, it is becoming more and

---

35 Of course, if your credit customers are not paying, any kind of lending could lead to disaster!

36 It is customary for the dealers selling and financing the equipment to assign the loan papers to a finance company who will be the real purchase money lender. So, although you deal with XYZ Dealer, your lender will be the bank or a finance company.

more common for even the non-equipment vendor to require a personal guarantee, and sometimes this personal guarantee is hidden in the credit application.[37]

Read the credit application!! I can't stress how important that is. Try to use some of the strategies I discuss in this Book to lessen the financial exposure.

---

37 I have seen situations where the bookkeeper of the business who had no ownership interest signed the credit application, not being aware that the fine print made anyone signing on behalf of the company personally liable for all of the company's debt to the vendor.

C H A P T E R   5

PERSONAL GUARANTEES

The personal guarantee of a loan or an account can cause enormous adverse financial harm to the guarantor in the event of a default by the entity or person whose loan is being guaranteed. Notwithstanding this fact, many of my clients never read the personal guarantees they sign, and in some cases don't even know they have guaranteed the indebtedness. Let's explore personal guarantees.

Bank Guarantees

As an initial question, why do lenders require personal guarantees? If the bank has properly underwritten the loan, one would think that the bank's collateral would be sufficient to satisfy the loan if the borrower defaults. If the collateral value is greatly in excess of the loan amount, that may be true, but the lender almost always still wants the borrower's attention and help in the event of a default where the bank has to liquidate the collateral. The way to get this attention and help is to require a personal guarantee. On the other hand, as discussed in more detail below, if the guarantor is wealthy or has plenty of assets, the bank can decide not to pursue the collateral, but instead to sue the guarantor.

Thus, in almost all small business loans made by a bank, the bank will require a personal guarantee. Let's suppose that your small business is borrowing $500,000 from the bank and is pledging its accounts receivable, inventory and equipment as collateral for the loan. If you are asked to personally guarantee the loan, don't feel that the lender will never call on you to pay even if the value of the collateral may be several times the amount of the loan. What would the value of the collateral be if the business had to shut down and be liquidated? It might be substantially less than the $500,000, and if the bank cannot be paid from the collateral, it will look to the guarantor to pay the difference—which in lender jargon is called the "deficiency".

On the other hand, and as discussed elsewhere in this Book, lenders never do a really good job of liquidating collateral. Therefore, if the financial condition of the guarantors is strong, the lender may decide not to bother with liquidation of the collateral, but instead sue the guarantors on the note obligation. In most states it is the lender's prerogative to first sue the guarantor before going after the collateral. That choice is usually dictated by a number of factors including whether the state law favors getting a judgment against the guarantor first before the bank liquidates the collateral and, of course, how strong the guarantor's personal financial situation is. [38]

It goes without saying that it makes a lot of sense to take the guarantee requirement very seriously even if the lender's representative tells you that the lender will never call on you to pay because the business has plenty of collateral. [39] You can see that personally guaranteeing a large loan can be financially ruinous to the guarantor if the business fails.

A smart lender will generally try to get the guarantor/principal of the borrower to liquidate the collateral. The guarantor/principal usually can get a much better price for the physical collateral like inventory and

---

38 Thus, the bank can simply opt to go after the guarantor and liquidate the collateral only if it is necessary.

39 There are cases in a number of state courts where the banker has insisted that the bank would never call on the guarantor to pay if there was a default. These statements are generally not enforceable, although there is an occasional case where the evidence is sufficient to support avoiding the guarantee.

equipment and also can do a lot better than the lender in collecting the accounts receivable.

Personal guarantees come in all different forms, but the worst from a borrower's standpoint is the bank form guarantee. The bank's well-paid (and well-heeled) lawyers have taken advantage of every waiver permitted by law. This means that the guarantor agrees in the form guarantee (also called a "guaranty") to waive all statutory and other guarantor defenses. Some of these defenses could, if not waived, save the day for a guarantor. What if the bank decides not to repossess or foreclose its collateral? The guarantor's liability is obviously increased. What if the bank gets little or nothing when it disposes of the collateral? The guarantor's liability is obviously increased. Get the idea? Both of these can be guarantor defenses under many state laws, and in some cases a bar to recovery by the bank. Bank lawyers are having a field day to see who can come up with a new waiver which will further strangle the guarantor!

One of the most interesting guarantor waivers is a waiver of using any defense that the business has. For example, your company has an account with a vendor. You guaranteed the account. Your business buys $10,000 of goods from the vendor. Upon receipt of the goods, you realize that some of the goods are "non-conforming," meaning they are defective or are not what you ordered. You advise the vendor which denies that the goods are non-conforming. The vendor sues your company and you. You and the company defend the lawsuit claiming the goods are non-conforming. The vendor files a motion to strike *your* defense on the grounds that you waived your right to use the business' defense. The court strikes your defense (but not the business'). This waiver has been held to be enforceable in a number of states.

There are defenses that are governed by the Uniform Commercial Code which can't be waived by the borrower. For example, if the bank does not dispose of its collateral in a commercially reasonable manner, the failure to do so will result in the court or jury determining what the real value of the collateral was at the time it was repossessed and giving the borrower and maybe the guarantor a credit for this value rather than the value which the bank had obtained in its sale. Unfortunately for guarantors, case law all over the country in recent years seems to be going in the direction of enforcing waivers by a guarantor even if the Uniform Commercial Code makes them unenforceable against the borrower.

Bank guarantees are also extremely broad in that they usually cover liability for the business' overdrafts, and other debts incurred with other departments of the bank. They may even cover liabilities owed to affiliates of the bank. For example, suppose that your business has a line of credit with Bad Bank, N.A., and you personally guaranteed the debt. Let's suppose that the business also has truck financing with a wholly owned affiliate of the bank, the Bad Truck Financing Company. Don't be surprised if the guarantee agreement also covers that debt—and the guarantee may not even specifically list Bad Truck Financing Company. Instead, the guarantee agreement will simply state that it covers any debts of the business (called sometimes, the "principal obligor") to any affiliate of the bank.

It follows from our discussion that bank form guarantees are hard to defeat in court. They are incredibly broad, and they contain so many waivers and other protections of the bank that it is almost impossible to defend against them. Only where the banker who prepares the guarantee form makes a mistake in filling in the form is there at least some defense available to the borrower.

Vendor Guarantees

Over the years I have been most successful in defeating vendor guarantees. These are guarantees which are usually found in the initial credit application that the small business gives to a vendor of goods or services. Often times the language creating the guarantee is hidden in the "fine print" of a credit application, and many times the guarantor doesn't even know that he or she has signed a guarantee. The forms used are different with every vendor, and many times use sloppy language and sometimes are filled out incorrectly. Under the laws of most, if not all states, a guarantee of debts has to be in writing. This is a carry-over from English law where a "Statute of Frauds" invalidated certain types of transactions if they were not in writing. One of the types of transactions which are required to be in writing is the guarantee of some other persons' debt.[40]

Thus, if the guarantee form does not name the proper parties or contains other "scrivener" errors, it may not be enforceable. On the other hand, some states allow these errors to be corrected by allowing the jury or judge to hear testimonial evidence of the creditor and debtor to explain what was really intended. Another common error in vendor guarantees is that they often-times do not contain waivers of defenses as are almost always set forth in the bank form guarantee. This can result in some very interesting litigation where the guarantor is able to defend by asserting what are normally statutory "surety" defenses like "increase of risk" to defeat the guarantee. "Increase of risk" was mentioned earlier and means that the vendor has done something like increasing the line of vendor credit to the business buyer without the guarantor's consent.

Strategies

There are several strategies to help make the personal guarantee less egregious. First, if the collateral at a **liquidation value** should be enough to pay off the debt, the guarantor can try to negotiate what is called a "**bad boy**" guarantee. A "bad boy" (or "bad girl") guarantee provides that as long as the guarantor and borrower do not do anything which would hinder the ability of the lender to liquidate the collateral, the guarantor will not be personally liable for the debt.[41] Not unexpectedly the common bad boy guarantee also provides that the guarantor will be liable in the event of any fraudulent misrepresentations or conduct. Thus, if the borrower and

---

40 Defenses under the Statute of Frauds are also available in the case of bank guarantees.

41 An example of a "trigger" action would be if the borrower filed Chapter 11 or if the borrower tried to get an injunction against the lender to prevent the lender from liquidating its collateral.

guarantor have misrepresented the amount of accounts receivable or their financial wherewithal, the guarantor will be viewed as a "bad boy" and will be liable for any deficiency.

Another strategy is to place a limit on the amount of debt for which the guarantor is responsible. A bank, finance company or vendor may be more likely to allow this type of guarantee than the bad boy. But be careful. The guarantee may seem to limit the guarantor's exposure to a certain amount, but in reality, the limitation turns out not to be as good as expected. For example, a guarantee that is capped at $250,000 may add accrued and unpaid interest and statutory or actual attorneys' fees and collection costs to the capped amount.[42] There also may be language that the amount guaranteed is the last $250,000 after credit for the liquidation of the collateral.

Capping the guaranteed amount works very well with vendor guarantees because it is usually much easier to negotiate with the vendor. But beware. The smart vendor, when seeing that the credit line exceeds the cap amount of the guarantee, will often times try to obtain a new application with no cap or an increased cap. A more troublesome strategy employed by the smart vendor is to add language to the form credit application that the capped amount is automatically increased if the credit limit is exceeded.

Another strategy for the guarantor is to provide that the guarantee terminates after a specified period of time. This is very useful with guarantees of long-term business premises leases, and I also recommend it with vendor guarantees. The logic is that after the business demonstrates to the lessor or the vendor that it is credit-worthy, then there is no further need for a guarantee. An "add-on" to this type of limitation is to have an automatic reduction in exposure over a period of time. So, for example, the initial exposure would be for the full amount, then it reduces by 1/3 for each of the next calendar years until the guarantee terminates. But you won't get any of these benefits if you don't ask!

---

42 Thus, a $250,000.00 "cap" may quickly turn into $305,000.00 when a years' unpaid interest at the 12% default rate ($30,000.00) plus another 10 % or so in attorneys' fees ($25,000.00) is added.

Finally, if there are several guarantors (e.g., partners in the business), it is a good idea to ask the lender if the lender will permit the guarantors to be liable **severally** and not **jointly and severally**. This is legalese, but it is important legalese! The normal guarantee with multiple guarantors makes each guarantor liable for 100% of the debt, i.e., "jointly and severally." Obviously, the wealthiest guarantor is going to be the target of the bank or vendor. A "several" guarantee makes each guarantor liable for a percentage of the debt which depends on the number of guarantors. So, if there are 3 guarantors, each guarantor can discharge his or her obligations to the bank or vendor by paying 1/3, and if the other guarantors don't pay, there is no additional liability for the guarantor who does pay.

Where there are going to be multiple guarantors, it is extremely important to know who your partners are and what their financial wherewithal is. I can't tell you how many clients I have had over the years who turned out to be the only one of multiple guarantors who had any financial ability to satisfy the indebtedness owed the lender. In one case the borrower had four partners, one of which was the manager of the company, and the others were supposed passive investors. The managing partner ran the company into the ground. He had little or no financial ability to satisfy the debt or make contributions of capital to keep the business going. The bank and other creditors were certainly going to look to the other three partners. Thankfully, the three remaining partners were able to sell the business and pay off the creditors.

Spousal Guarantees

Lenders also like to have the spouse of the principal of the small business to guarantee the debt—even if the spouse has no involvement with the business. In most cases the lender requires the "innocent spouse" to guarantee the debt along with the principal of the business so that the bank can put more leverage on the principal if there is a default. There is a federal law known as the Equal Credit Opportunity Act of 1974 which used to protect spouses whose guarantees were not needed to supply financial wherewithal but were nevertheless required by the lender. Unfortunately, recent case law has watered down the usefulness of this statute as a defense. If you have a situation which might be covered by "ECOA, contact a commercial lawyer who is knowledgeable in this area of the law.

Always resist any request by the bank to make your spouse or other family member a guarantor of a commercial indebtedness.

Pledging Your Residence

Many lenders also will require the principal of the small business to pledge his or her personal residence[43] as collateral. If the house is jointly owned by the principal and his or her spouse, most lenders may require that the spouse of the principal pledge his or her interest in their home as security. Unless the spouse has signed a full personal guarantee, the spouse will not be personally liable, but the pledge of the spouse's share of the house makes the house available for the lender to foreclose in the event of default.

No one should have to pledge his/her/their home to secure a business loan. If a lender requires this, it is only for the purpose of obtaining leverage over the guarantor, and you should shop the loan and find another lender. **Avoid this in every way that you can.** Remember *the bank is not your friend*, and I can guarantee that if there is any recoverable equity in your home, the lender will take your home if it can't get paid through liquidation of the business' assets or other means.

Unfortunately, if the small business is a start-up and has little or no assets of value to pledge or if there is any weakness in the financial health of the small business, the small business is not going to be able to obtain a loan without pledging all of the business' assets plus assets of the owners,

---

43 Believe it or not, your government through the Small Business Administration regularly requires the pledging of personal residences in SBA backed loans. Apparently, the government doesn't subscribe to Sir Edward Coke's statement that "the house of everyone is to him as his Castle and Fortress." This saying has been modernized to say, "a man's or woman's home is his/her castle."

including spouses. At that time, the borrower's leverage with the lender is very small. I have seen some of the worst secured loans and unconscionable guarantees occur when the small business is a start-up or is suffering. If you can be objective—and this is very difficult—decide whether you and your family would be better off **not** borrowing the money.

One other comment about pledging your personal residence. I was involved in a case years ago where some astute developers were required to personally guarantee large commercial loans which they used to build office buildings and shopping centers. These people were very wealthy and very successful. They therefore had some leverage with their lender-banks who were delighted to make the large loans as long as they had personal guarantees. These developers were able to put a provision in their personal guarantees which excepted out their personal residences, consumer assets like automobiles, furniture and even antiques and paintings and a certain amount of cash from possible levy by the lender-banks if there was a default in the loans, and the lender-banks obtained judgments against the guarantors. I have not seen this type of limited guarantee agreed to by lenders in recent times, although as pointed out earlier, I have seen numerous "bad boy/girl" guarantees.

Credit Card Debt

When a business takes out a "company credit card" with a credit card company, each card that is issued has an individual's name on it. The credit card company is generally eager to issue as many company credit cards as you want. Thus, the CEO may have a company credit card, and salespeople may also have them to use for travel and entertaining customers. Perhaps even spouses of the owners of the business may have company credit cards. Beware! Everyone whose name is on a credit card is personally liable for the charges he or she makes on the card if the company defaults in paying the credit card debt.

As we will discuss later regarding "alter ego" issues, it is never a good idea to mix business debt with personal debt. Spouses and family members who don't work in the business should not be issued company credit cards. Some of the worst individual cases I have handled involve a salesperson for a company which files a bankruptcy. The company cannot pay the credit card indebtedness which now is the liability of each of the persons who have company credit cards. The poor salesperson has been flying all over, staying in hotels and entertaining customers. The salesperson's credit card debt is huge. If you are such a person, a better way to handle company credit card debt would be not to wait until the bill comes in to get paid, but instead, submit weekly requests for reimbursement.

Caveats

Caveat is a Latin word which means *warning*. In this Chapter I have discussed possible strategies which might lessen the personal liability which arises from a personal guarantee. I have also shown you how personal guarantees can result in financial ruin for the guarantor. Below I have listed certain "rules" to follow regarding personal guarantees.

1. **Never guarantee a debt where a personal guarantee was not initially required**.

If at all possible, never guarantee a debt to the bank where the bank has lent money to your company and did not require a guarantee when the loan was made. Why give the bank what essentially is additional collateral when it didn't originally request it? What is the reason for the bank's request? If it is because the bank has now determined that your company is in financial extremis, **don't do it!** You will find that the Special Assets Department is going to treat your company's workout the same way irrespective of whether you guarantee the debtor or not. You will be giving the bank a large gift for essentially no consideration.

Of course, it may be that you are asking for an increase in the loan amount which exceeds what the bank would loan you without a guarantee. If that is the case, try to negotiate a cap on your personal liability or a "bad boy/girl guarantee"—discussed previously. After all, the bank originally agreed to loan your company a certain amount of money *without* a personal guarantee. At the very least, insist that the guarantee only cover the additional sum.

2. **Never guarantee a debt of a financially troubled company.**

As an example, suppose that your company is having financial difficulties and is in default on a bank loan or is near default. In my experience unless there is a reasonable possibility of working out the debt *so that the company can continue in operation in the same way it has previously*—which is generally not going to happen—guaranteeing a debt of a company which is going down is foolhardy and may result in a financial disaster for the guarantor. If the bank is going to liquidate the company or not renew the loan, why should you personally guarantee the loan so that now your personal assets will be at risk?

Look realistically at whether your company is viable. Is your personal guarantee going to buy another six months after which it will fail and be liquidated—along with you!

Don't complicate your ability to start again. You have a good chance to come back after a failure. Believe it or not, my experience over many years is that even though an entrepreneur may lose his or her company or have to file bankruptcy, there is a good chance that he or she will be back, start a new business and will flourish. It is the American way!

The reason is because entrepreneurs are risk takers. Notwithstanding the fact that small business entrepreneurs have an uphill battle to success because of federal and state laws which favor the banks and other lenders, entrepreneurs continue to take risks and create viable businesses which employ more people than all the mega-companies. In short, small businesses and the entrepreneurs which start and own them and are what makes the American economy go. If you are prudent and don't take ridiculous risks, there is every reason to believe that you will be able to launch a come-back.

As an example of the resilience of entrepreneurs, I had a client many years ago who lost everything in the failure of his business. Years later through hard work and skill he retired with a net worth of hundreds of millions of dollars, many tens of millions dollars of which he has given away to charities. **Never lose hope!**

3. **Never guarantee a debt if the debt guaranteed is so much that you will be ruined financially if the bank has to enforce the guarantee.**

I have never understood why anyone would guarantee a debt over and above what he or she could afford to pay if the company failed. Let's look at an example. Suppose "Headstone Company," which makes headstones borrows $ 1 million from the bank. Mary, the owner of the company, has $500,000.00 in personal assets other than the value of her ownership in Headstone Company. The loan will be used to purchase blank headstone inventory and to cover operating expenses. Headstone Company pledges its inventory and accounts receivable to the bank to secure the loan. The bank requires an unlimited personal guarantee. Once the loan is made, Mary figures that she will have about $1.5 million in inventory, and she has back orders for product. Things appear to be very rosy for Headstone Company and Mary—at least that's what her banker told her at a lunch at the fancy restaurant he took her.

In order to underwrite the loan, Mary's banker had to write a memo to the credit file showing how the bank would get out of the loan if there was a default. The memo says that the inventory would be worth $750,000.00 if there is a default and the outstanding accounts receivable which it also has a security interest in would be worth $500,000.00. But the banker is not in the business of making headstones and has little or no experience in the industry. **Before signing the personal guarantee, Mary should evaluate her risk if the company fails.**

First of all, Mary knows that if she has to close the business, her blank headstone inventory is worth 25 cents on the dollars because of the high cost of transportation of the headstones to another dealer and because of the competitive nature of her business—none of which the banker knows. Put another way she knows—but the banker doesn't—that if she had to close the business, her inventory of $1.5 million would probably have been depleted to a level of not more that $1 million. Unfortunately, the $1 million of inventory would be only worth around $250,000.00 at liquidation. She figures that outstanding receivables owed mostly by funeral homes would shrink to $250,000.00 and, about half of that ($125,000) would be collectible.

So, Mary knows—if she takes the time to analyze her risk before borrowing the $1 million from the bank—that if Headstone Company has financial difficulties and has to be liquidated, the bank "on a good day" will recover $375,000.00 less the costs of liquidation, and that she will be responsible for the other $625,000.00 because of her personal guarantee. Mary also knows that her $500,000.00 in assets are not liquid, and it would be difficult to turn them into cash. She will likely have to file an individual bankruptcy or a small business Chapter 11.

Is it really worth it for Mary to borrow the $1 million from the bank? Perhaps, it is. But wouldn't it be prudent for Mary to at least try to negotiate a "bad girl guarantee" or at least a guarantee with a capped amount that she knows that she can afford without being driven into bankruptcy?

4. **Finally, as I discussed earlier in this Chapter, never, never, never pledge your personal residence to secure a guarantee of the company's loan; and never agree to a guarantee by your spouse or another family member who is not involved in the business.**

FORECLOSURE AND REPOSSESSION OF COLLATERAL

Personal Property

Most businesspeople have at least heard of the so-called "repo man" in the context of the repossession of consumer vehicles or even household goods. The owner of the vehicle defaults in his or her installment payments, and the bank decides to repossess its collateral. The "repo man" comes to wherever the vehicle is parked and hauls it off using a wrecker. What happens next, is not necessarily widely known. The bank must now dispose of the automobile. One of the esoteric concepts of secured lending is that at this point, although the bank has possession of the automobile, *it does not have title to it*, and therefore the bank is not the owner of the vehicle. What it does have is the right to *dispose* of the vehicle, usually by sale.

In most states the rules set forth in the Uniform Commercial Code, discussed below, govern how the bank proceeds with disposing of its collateral. In order to comply with the law, the bank generally has to give notice to the owner of an imminent sale. In some states this allows the owner of the vehicle to "redeem" it by paying off the indebtedness.[44] With vehicles, the next step is usually to take the vehicle to a wholesale auto auction and sell it to the highest bidder. If the vehicle is a very expensive one, the bank may well try to sell it to one of its other customers. Whatever the bank gets for the vehicle, less its cost of repossession and sale, is credited against the owner's debt. If there is any significant deficiency—and there almost always is when automobiles are repossessed—then the former owner is liable to the bank for the deficiency.

Foreclosure of commercial personal property collateral is similar to what is described above for vehicles, but it can be a fairly complicated process. In the great majority of states, it is almost entirely governed by Article 9 of the Uniform Commercial Code which, as previously indicated, is known as the "UCC."[45] How foreclosure works depends on what type of personal property collateral is being foreclosed. Physical or hard assets such as inventory or equipment can be repossessed by the secured creditor through what is known as "self-help", i.e., the secured creditor or his agent (the "repo man") goes out and actually takes physical possession of the asset and removes it from the borrower's premises. Most states also have statutory procedures in which a court can issue an order directing the sheriff or other court officer to take possession of the particular piece of collateral. In some states this order is called a "writ of possession" or a "writ of attachment." There are also state laws which permit a court to appoint a receiver to take possession of the collateral and to actually sell it. As in the case of a vehicle, even though the bank has possession of its personal property collateral, *it does not own* it, but has the legal authority to *dispose* of it.

Lender repossession and sale of commercial collateral is a terrible way to dispose of the bank's collateral. Seldom does the lender obtain

---

44 In my home state of Georgia, when a titled vehicle is involved, the notice must contain certain information and must be sent to the owner within a certain amount of time. If the lender fails to comply with these procedures, it forfeits its right to collect a deficiency from the owner. Beware, this forfeiture provision is unusual and may not be applicable in your state.

45 Please note that some limited types of personal property—generally crops, livestock and vehicles—may, depending on the particular state, be governed by separate laws, or a combination of the UCC and other laws.

anywhere close to the value of the collateral. Inventory may bring ten cents on the dollar, and equipment may bring anywhere from twenty-five to fifty cents on the dollar. Furniture and office fixtures may not even bring ten percent of their cost—even if they are relatively new. Computers and IT equipment may bring next to nothing.[46]

There is no way to "take possession" of non-physical assets such as accounts receivable. The UCC permits a creditor with a security interest in accounts receivable to *collect* the accounts directly.[47] The process involves the secured creditor notifying the account debtors to pay the creditor rather than the borrower. This is generally not an efficient way for the lender to collect the accounts because account debtors don't trust the process and may refuse to pay, and the lender really has no way to deal with claims for defective goods, services or credits.

As I have suggested elsewhere in this Book, unless the lender has made mistakes in documenting the loan, the lender has a great deal of leverage over the borrower when it comes to repossession, disposition of the collateral and assessment of a deficiency against the borrower. I will discuss deficiencies later in this Chapter. However, at the point in time where the lender is moving toward repossession of its collateral, the borrower does have a degree of leverage based on the borrower's better ability to maximize collections of accounts receivable and sale of inventory and other collateral. The leverage increases if the lender knows that the borrower, individually, will not be able to satisfy any significant deficiency—which is very likely to occur if the lender collects the receivables and sells off the physical collateral. Conversely, the borrower's leverage decreases if there is a lot of equity in the collateral over and above the debt, and the collateral can be sold at a forced sale for at least the amount of the debt.

---

46 Years ago, I represented a bank which repossessed a three-year-old computer system. The bank had lent the owner $500,000.00 to purchase the system. The bank sold it at private sale for $500.00.

47 The UCC does allow the lender to sell the accounts receivable in bulk, but this remedy is seldom used for obvious reasons, i.e., the "bottom feeder" buyer will pay next to nothing for them.

A savvy lender will try to work with the borrower and allow the borrower to deal with the account debtors because using the Borrower to collect the accounts is a much more efficient way of collecting them and maximizing recovery for the lender. Unless the lender is inept, it will likely negotiate with the borrower on the amount of a deficiency.

So, let's consider a hypothetical. Suppose the borrower is a wholesale hardware business. It purchases hardware from its vendors and sells it to retailers. It borrows $500,000 from the bank and gives the bank a security interest in the inventory, which at cost is valued at $300,000, and a security interest in accounts receivable which has a face value of $500,000. The borrower defaults, and the bank wants to dispose of its collateral. The borrower will be liquidated, so there is no ability for the borrower to repay the bank after repossession. The guarantors have little or no personal assets, or their personal assets are not near enough to result in payment of debt. If the bank repossesses the inventory and sells it at private sale, it will likely get $50,000 for it. If the bank employs a collection agency to collect the accounts receivable, it will have to pay the collection agency's contingent fee of, let's say, 20 % of net collections, and importantly, because neither the bank, nor the collection agency can resolve defective inventory and warranty claims—without the borrower's help—it is likely that the collection agency will have to give the account debtors discounts.

It is easy to see that collecting even 50 % after paying the fees of the collection agency would be a good result. Thus, the bank will recover $50,000 for the inventory and $250,000 from collection of the accounts receivable—which quite honestly is high. So, on a $500,000 original debt secured by collateral worth $800,000, the bank only collects $300,000. On the other hand, if the bank makes a deal with the borrower to sell the inventory and collect the accounts receivable, the result could be a much higher recovery for the bank, and less of a deficiency for the guarantors to deal with.

It deserves repeating: *negotiate early with the bank*. The strategy, therefore, is for the borrower to cut a deal on the deficiency with the bank when the borrower has the leverage, and not *after* the liquidation of the bank's collateral. The borrower will have no leverage after the liquidation of the collateral, and the bank will really have no incentive to discount the amount of the deficiency.[48]

Real Property

Just as real estate mortgage documents are different in each state, so is the procedure for foreclosing real property collateral. Some states require a court to be involved in the process, while others have "non-judicial" foreclosure procedures where no court is involved in the process. Other states have both non-judicial and judicial foreclosure procedures, thereby enabling the lender to take its choice in how it will foreclose.

Where court action is required, the lender generally must first institute a suit against the borrower and guarantors. A court will approve foreclosure, and if the lender wants to pursue a deficiency, the court will determine the fair market value of the property and require that amount to be credited against the debt. At that point, the court will enter judgment against the borrower and guarantors. It is very important that you employ a competent lawyer to help you through a foreclosure since every state's laws are different.

The non-judicial foreclosure process is quick and has much less in the way of due process safeguards. Generally, the property is advertised in the county legal newspaper—one most businesspeople have never heard of—for several weeks and then at some time after it is advertised, the lender will "sell" the property, usually at the courthouse steps or other loca-tion prescribed by the foreclosure statute to the "highest bidder." Most of the time the lender will be the only bidder and become the owner because few people even know the property is being foreclosed and is for sale, and

---

48 I had a client once who would not follow my advice to make a deal first with the bank before he helped the bank liquidate the collateral. The banker urged the borrower to help the bank liquidate the collateral and told my client not to worry because the bank would treat him fairly on any deficien-cy. After the collateral, including inventory, equipment and accounts receivable, was liquidated, the bank sued the guarantor-owner for the deficiency. The guarantor's only remedy was to file bankruptcy. Remember, *the bank is not your friend*!

even if they do know there is not much time for a prospective bidder to conduct due diligence on the property and examine zoning, environmental and other issues which would affect value. It is easy to see that a foreclosure auction on the courthouse steps or wherever is far from a commercially reasonable sale.

The bid price is what is credited against the debt to determine the deficiency. **It is not the price that the lender gets for the property when it actually puts the property on the real estate market after the foreclosure.** Many lenders will have the property appraised before the foreclosure sale and will bid the property in at the appraised value. Other unscrupulous lenders will "low-ball" their bid, especially if the borrower or guarantors of the debt are financially sound. The idea is that the lender can get title to the real estate *and* pursue the borrower and/or guarantors for the fabricated deficiency.

In many instances after foreclosure, especially with income producing property, a lender will transfer ownership of the property to a subsidiary[49] of the lender which will continue to lease the property until market conditions improve. At that point the subsidiary will sell the property on the market for a price that may even be *more* than the debt owed by the borrower. Unfortunately, the borrower and guarantors do not get the benefit of the profit.

Deficiencies

As discussed above, most of the time foreclosure of personal property or real estate will not yield enough to pay off the debt and will leave a "deficiency." As indicated above, this is the amount still owing by the borrower and guarantors after getting a credit for the proceeds of the liquidation— less costs and attorneys' fees. The UCC specifies in detail how a secured creditor is to foreclose its personal property collateral. As we have discussed

---

49 In the vernacular of the lending industry, the properties placed into these special purpose subsidiaries are call "REO" properties—which stands for "real estate owned."

earlier, it requires the lender to give certain notices to the Borrower and Guarantors and to dispose of the collateral in a "commercially reasonable manner." As we have seen, physical collateral can either be disposed of by public auction or private sale. In either case the secured creditor may be required to advertise the sale in order to act in a commercially reasonable manner. If the secured creditor does not follow the rules required by the UCC, then any deficiency may be contested by the borrower and guarantors in a deficiency suit filed by the lender. Of course, as discussed in my chapter on personal guarantees, the guarantors may have waived their rights to contest any deficiency based on the creditor's failure to follow these rules.

Obtaining a deficiency against the borrower and guarantors when *real estate* is foreclosed is handled differently in every state, and as discussed above, may involve a completely different procedure than the foreclosure of personal property. In some states there is a bar to collection of a deficiency if certain kinds of real estate like residential property are foreclosed or if the real estate is foreclosed non-judicially.[50] Unfortunately, most states *do* allow a deficiency to be collected by the lender.

As discussed above, if collection of a deficiency is permitted, there may be safeguards which require that the lender credit the debt with the fair market value of the real estate irrespective of whether that was the amount obtained at the foreclosure sale. These safeguards are very important in non-judicial foreclosures because as I have suggested the "auction sale" conducted on the courthouse steps will never bring the fair market value and could result in the creditor buying the property at an unreasonably low amount.

In my home state of Georgia, the legislature during the Great Depression of the 1930's enacted a "confirmation" statute which required court involvement after non-judicial foreclosure, as a prerequisite to the assessment of a deficiency. It was enacted to keep unscrupulous lenders

---

50 Some states do not allow deficiencies on purchase money real estate loans where the seller finances the purchase of the real estate. However, these "bar statutes" do not apply to bank financing of the purchase.

from swindling farmers by foreclosing their farms and bidding them in at the foreclosure sale for much less than fair market value and then suing the poor farmers for a made-up deficiency. After nearly eighty years on the books and after being used thousands of times, the Georgia Courts essentially repealed the statute several years ago by holding that the statute could be waived by borrowers and guarantors. The result is that there are no longer, in my opinion, any safeguards in Georgia against unscrupulous lenders in real estate foreclosures. To make matters worse, after a number of tries, members of the Georgia legislature who favored enacting safeguards could not get the votes necessary to enact remedial legislation, probably because of the strong arm of the bank and lender lobby. There is no doubt that the Georgia Legislature is not a small business owner's friend![51]

When borrowers are faced with imminent foreclosure, some will employ legal counsel to attempt to enjoin the foreclosure by going into state or federal court seeking an injunction against the lender. I have found that most of the time if the documentation of the loan is valid and default is easily proven, this is a big waste of time and money. Unfortunately, this leaves only bankruptcy as an alternative to stop the foreclosure. Whether or not to file a bankruptcy is a big decision. In my chapters on bankruptcy and Chapter 11, I discuss some of the considerations of why and when you should consider bankruptcy.

In sum foreclosure by a secured creditor is a harsh remedy, and the potential adverse effect of foreclosure on the borrower and the guarantor of a loan is extremely large. As I have suggested before, it is imperative for any small business owners who are facing foreclosure to employ competent counsel with experience in commercial matters to help the owners decide how to protect themselves.

---

51 There are similar statutes in other states which may provide that a borrower's rights to court supervision of the foreclosure cannot be waived. Check your own state law!

ASSET PROTECTION AND FRAUDULENT OR VOIDABLE TRANSFERS

I decided to include the discussion of asset protection in the same chapter I discuss fraudulent and voidable transfers because the remedy for creditors (or a trustee in bankruptcy) of a debtor engaged in an unlawful asset protection scheme is to institute suit against the person receiving the transfer of assets to undo the fraudulent or voidable transfer. Setting aside the transfer means that the court voids it and returns title to the asset to its original owner. If the transferred asset has been sold by the transferee to a third party or involves money, then the creditor or trustee can seek a money judgment against the transferee.[52] In fact if the third-party buyer had reason to know about the transfer, he or she can also be sued.

I frankly do not like using the term, "*Asset Protection*," because it implies that the debtor is doing something unlawful like preventing a creditor to whom he or she owes money from exercising a legal right to take the debtor's assets to satisfy a legally owing debt by illegally hiding or transferring the assets in fraud of the creditor. If that is what you are intending, then you can rest assured that if the person threatening has a lawful right to your assets, your action in preventing him from taking your assets

---

52 The "transferor" is the person or entity which transfers the asset. The "transferee" is the person or entity which receives the asset from the transferor.

is likely a fraudulent or voidable transaction, and you will be making a very bad mistake.

Nevertheless, I am going to use the term, "Asset Protection" from time to time because its meaning is generally understood by the business public.

Estate Planning

Almost every wealthy person employs professionals to devise and create "estate planning" strategies. These estate planning strategies usually involve a combination of wills, trusts and limited liability companies (or corporations) along with significant transfers of assets among the trusts and limited liability companies (or corporations). The purpose of these devices is always to shield the assets of the wealthy individual from estate taxes and allow these assets to be transferred to the wealthy individual's family with the least amount of tax. There is generally nothing illegal about the creation and use of these strategies because the wealthy person still has the financial wherewithal after implementing the strategies to pay all of his or her existing and future creditors. For the wealthy, smart estate planning, when done properly and timely, has a secondary benefit of asset protection.

Importantly, the current tax laws already shield the vast number of Americans from estate tax liability.[53] Thus, much of these "estate planning" devices have no purpose or effect on ninety-nine percent of Americans because when they die, the value of their estate is less—and usually much less—than the amount the government allows to be excluded from the payment of estate taxes. Thus "estate planning" for most Americans is really a misnomer and is in reality either an asset protection device or involves the transfer of assets during the life of the transferor rather that through a will after death.

That is not to say, however, that middle class Americans do not need wills. Wills provide for the assets of the deceased person to be transferred

---

53 At the time this Book was written, under federal law, the estate tax exemption per individual is $11.7 million and for married couples, $23.4 million.

to the beneficiary or beneficiaries of his or her choice. A person without a will risks the likelihood that the laws of his or her state will govern who receives these assets. So, for example, state law may determine that assets will be split among a person's children and spouse instead of all of the assets going to a person's spouse. Simple wills are generally cheap, and even can be prepared by the person himself or herself without the help of a lawyer. There are a number of legitimate online services on the internet, and a good many publications available at bookstores or online.

So, is asset protection against the law? It is not against the law as long as it is done timely, not with the intent to defraud existing and future creditors and does not in fact defraud creditors. The words, "timely," and "intent" are the keys. For example, some people, married or single, may want to distribute some of their assets to their family members *before they die*. Subject to the laws governing fraudulent or voidable transfers, there is nothing wrong with these transfers, and these transfers are really not asset protection devices, but *inter vivos* estate planning. *Inter vivos* is a Latin phrase which means "during one's lifetime."

Put another way, a person who has no financial difficulties and is timely paying his creditors may employ strategies regarding the transfers of his or her assets which could have the effect of later protecting his or her assets from creditors in the event such a person suffers unexpected financial difficulties in the future.

However, asset protection through estate planning does **not** work where the estate planning takes place *after* the person begins suffering financial difficulties. This simple truth seems hard for many people and frankly, some lawyers to understand. However, it is really nothing more than common sense. Consider the following factual scenario:

Jack lost his business through no fault of his own during the Covid pandemic. Over many years he had accumulated a nice nest egg of assets. Unfortunately, he owes the bank and other creditors more than these assets are worth. He has never engaged in estate planning or asset protection other than having a simple will.

Prior to his creditors beginning to sue him, Jack decides to transfer many of these assets to his wife, Jill, and to their children Jack, Jr. and Mary, in order to keep them out of reach of his creditors. Does the law permit Jack to do this? His family is not buying the assets, and so Jack will receive nothing of value in exchange for the contemplated transfers.

Common sense would say no. Jack cannot transfer his assets out of the reach of his creditors because creditors have a right to rely on a debtor's assets to get paid. Thus, hiding or transferring assets to hinder and delay creditors constitutes fraud in every state. Many states have adopted the Uniform Voidable Transactions Act[54] which prohibits this type of transfer and enables a defrauded creditor to undo or set aside the transfer and take the asset or recover a judgment for the value of the asset from the transferee. Similarly, the federal bankruptcy code also allows fraudulent transfers to be set aside or "avoided."

Let's change the facts. Jack is a successful businessman. Over the years he has transferred some, but not all of his assets to his wife, Jill, and to his children, Jack, Jr. and Mary. Jack's intent in doing so is *inter vivos* estate planning (i.e., transferring assets while alive rather than after one's death). He received nothing from Jill or his children in exchange for the transfers. Before and after the transfers, he has plenty of assets left with which to pay his creditors, and he was doing so. Many years after the transfers, John's business fails, and he will not be able to pay his creditors in full. May his creditors recover the assets or the value of the assets which he transferred to his family?

The answer is probably not. If the intent of the transferor is simply to accomplish some type of *inter vivos* estate planning, and the length of time between the transfers and the business failure is fairly long, it will be less likely that these transfers will be found to be fraudulent or voidable.[55]

---

54 Previously called the Uniform Fraudulent Transfers Act.

55 In many states, the statute of limitations for filing a state law voidable transactions suit is four years from the date of the transfer. But there is additional time added to the limitations period if the transfer is fraudulent and hidden.

However, these statutes are complicated, and I would urge anyone contemplating taking such action to seek professional help from a lawyer who is knowledgeable in creditors rights law.[56]

Another misunderstood dangerous device which some so-called asset protection advisors recommend is either to put all of a person's assets into some sort of trust for a spouse or children.[57] First of all, this is not going to work if the transferor (remember, the person doing the transferring) is having financial difficulties. Importantly, it is also not going to work if the person is transferring business assets and after the transfer his business is left with an "unreasonably small" capital base.

Let's consider an example. Dr. Cheatem's malpractice insurance is very expensive because of his medical specialty. He is in a state which does not require him to have malpractice insurance, or the state permits him to have a very small face amount. He and his asset protection advisor, N. Competent, Esq., decide that he should transfer all of his assets into a trust for his wife and children. The transfer will leave him with no assets at all. Further, his earnings from his practice will also go into the trust because he is structuring his practice so that the trust essentially owns his practice.

Here is what is going to happen to Dr. Cheatem and his family if he gets sued for malpractice and loses. If the trust receiving the assets is a *revocable* trust, that is, it can be terminated at will by Dr. Cheatem, the victim of his malpractice who recovers the judgment against Dr. Cheatem will be able to go after the assets in the *revocable* trust as if the trust didn't exist. If the trust is an *irrevocable* trust, the transfers can be set aside under the Uniform Voidable Transactions Act or the Bankruptcy Code subject to

---

56 I have represented people who sought advice from a lawyer who does not practice in the area of bankruptcy and creditors rights and who advised these people that it was OK to transfer their home to their spouse just prior to the failure of their business. This is just unbelievable to me! In some instances, the lawyer can be personally liable for aiding and abetting the fraud.

57 I have actually known lawyers who set up *offshore* trusts and entities to hold title to the assets. It just never ceases to amaze me how intelligent people can believe that these actions can be used legally to cheat creditors!

time limitations contained in both laws.[58] In fact, in a blatant fraud as this one, it is likely that the creditor or trustee may be able to recover punitive damages against Dr. Cheatem and perhaps even his lawyer.

It is common sense, and needs restating that when a person cannot pay his or her lawful debts, his or her creditors have the right to recover the unpaid indebtedness from so much of the person's assets that are not exempted by law from creditor recovery—e.g., IRA's and 401k plans. So, hiding assets from creditors by transferring them should be, and it is unlawful.

One rule I advise clients to use when they consider asset transfers is to step back and objectively look at the contemplated transaction, and ask: "Does this transaction defraud my creditors? Does it keep my creditors from collecting what they are owed?" Unless there is a state or federal law which would shield the contemplated transaction from creditors, then the answer to these questions should be enough for one to decide whether such a transfer is legitimate.

Protection of Assets Authorized by Federal and State Law

Other than lawful *inter vivos* transfers discussed above, are there other legitimate asset protections which can be employed to shield a person's assets from creditors? The answer is yes. Some of these protections may surprise you; others will not.

Many states have various state laws which protect certain assets from creditor enforcement actions. Other states, such as my home state of Georgia, have very few such laws, and many of them were reluctantly enacted to follow the mandate of federal law.

---

58 I once had a client who had gone to a wills and trust lawyer who advertised that he specialized in asset protection. He set up a multi-tiered structure of trusts to shield the client's assets from creditors. The client came to me when he began to suffer financial difficulties. During my interview with him, he told me that the lawyer had created so many trusts, that he did not know which of the many trust bank accounts to use to buy groceries. This client was an intelligent businessman, and it is impossible for me to understand how he could have thought that such an absurdity would work.

Tenants by the Entirety

The concept of "Tenants by the Entirety" comes from English law. In England, there were two ways that a married couple could own property: each could own the property separately, or they could own the property jointly. If they owned the property jointly, then the law recognized this ownership as a unique ownership, separate from their individual ownership. This was called Tenants by the Entirety ("TBE"). In states where TBE is enacted into law, TBE has a dramatic positive effect if one of the spouses has financial difficulties and suffers the entry of a judgment. The judgment will not encumber or adversely affect the TBE ownership of the property unless the other spouse is also a judgment debtor, i.e., the judgment was recovered against both of the spouses.

When this Book was written, twenty-five states and the District of Columbia recognized TBE in either personal property or real property or both. For example, a married couple may hold TBE ownership of both personal and real property in Florida, but only ownership in real property in North Carolina. Thus, a married couple in Florida can hold a joint bank account (personal property), own an automobile jointly (also personal property) and own real estate jointly—all protected as TBE.

On the other hand, in Georgia and twenty-four other states, there is no distinction between owning property—whether personal property or real property—jointly and through TBE. Therefore, there is no protection whatsoever to a married couple in Georgia in these states. In Georgia if a married couple's home is held jointly and a creditor recovers a judgment against the husband, the husband's share of the home will then be encumbered by the judgment, making it impossible for the couple to sell the home free and clear. Residency in a state recognizing TBE may not be required in order to take advantage of TBE. Thus, a Georgia married couple can own a Florida condominium as TBE.

But beware! If you are already having financial difficulties, transferring your assets into a TBE may not work because it still is hindering and defrauding your creditors by transferring assets which were available to satisfy creditors into a form of ownership which prevents creditors from pursuing the same assets. As you can see, timing is everything when considering transferring assets.

Limited Liability Companies

Again, remembering the rule that transferring assets when you are suffering financial difficulties is generally not going to work and will probably lead to worse problems, another asset protection device is to take advantage of state law prohibitions on the levying of a judgment against membership interests in a Limited Liability Company. You must check your state law before considering this device.[59] However, if your state is like most states, it prohibits the enforcing or satisfying of a judgment against a membership interest in an LLC. So, an asset can be transferred into an LLC owned by the transferor and his or her spouse, children or other family member. However, I want to stress again—but hopefully don't have to remind you—that if the transferor is having financial difficulties this device usually will not work and could be risky.[60] As I have suggested, anyone contemplating this type of asset strategy is well advised to seek competent legal advice.

Here is an example of the use of an LLC. Suppose a couple having no financial difficulties decides to purchase a small office building for their business. They decide to purchase it in the name of an LLC which they and their children will own as members. Later, the couple suffers financial difficulties. Can judgment creditors of the couple encumber or foreclose the office building? The answer is probably not. Creditors will generally

---

59 "Levy" is a legal term which means to enforce a judgment or the judgment lien against a property interest. How this is done is dependent on state law.

60 There are cases which hold that the transfer of money or real property into an LLC in exchange for membership interests in the LLC is still "hindering, delaying and defrauding creditors" because before the transfer a judgment creditor will have a lien on the real estate and the ability in many states of garnishing the bank account holding the cash.

not be able to force a sale of the office building or encumber it, but they can in most states obtain a "charging order" from a court which would require the LLC to turn over to the creditors any *distributions* paid out of the LLC to the judgment debtor.[61] Thus, if the LLC rents out part of the office building, any of the rental proceeds which are distributed to any of the members who are judgment debtors would be subject to the "charging order." Importantly, none of the distributions to the family members who are not judgment debtors would be affected.

Social Security, Pension and Retirement Plans

Federal law prohibits the garnishing or attachment of social security payments. However, the law does not prohibit an agency of the federal government, like the IRS or the U.S. Treasury Department from seizing all or part of the social security payments which are owed by a person who has unpaid obligations to the IRS or other governmental agency. Generally, these agencies will not take all of the social security, but they could.

Money and assets in federally approved pension and retirement plans like 401K plans, profit sharing plans and other similar devices, and money and assets in IRA plans and SEPs are protected from creditor enforcement under federal law and the laws of most states. Even bankruptcy law exempts these plans from becoming part of the assets of the bankruptcy estate which is distributed to creditors.

Depending on your state law, the *proceeds* of these plans may be treated differently. Thus, if you receive a payment from an IRA or 401K plan and deposit the payment into a bank account, all or a portion of that money may not be protected.

One important rule for you to follow if you are having financial difficulties is to use money from these protected pension and retirement funds *only as a last resort*. Do not use them to pay the bank or other creditors. The

---

61 "Judgment Debtor" is the person or entity which suffered the recovery of a judgment in court in a suit brought by the "judgment creditor."

bank and other creditors *cannot reach these assets*. Use these monies, only if you have to for living expenses.[62]

Homestead Exemptions

Every state has homestead exemptions. These laws had their origin as one of the first debtor protection statutes. They were enacted many years ago to protect borrowers. In general, a homestead exemption exempts certain types of assets from being encumbered by a judgment lien.[63] It does not protect the asset from being encumbered by a mortgage or a statutory lien like a mechanics' lien. State law may allow homestead exemptions in both personal and real property. A number of state laws exempt a person's residence. Other state laws only exempt a certain amount of equity in the person's residence.

In modern times most states have enacted homestead exemption statutes which apply only to a person's assets when he or she files a bankruptcy. Although the federal bankruptcy statute, as discussed earlier, is a uniform statute which applies to everyone no matter where the person lives, the entitlement of bankruptcy debtors to exempt certain assets from the bankruptcy is different from one state to another.

Thus, in Florida the homestead exemption will exempt a large portion of the equity in the person's residence, while in Georgia the exemption is quite low.

Litigation Involving Fraudulent Transfers

As discussed above, transfers of assets that are made to hinder, delay and defraud creditors or which are made when a debtor is insolvent

---

62 I speak to so many clients who have wasted these protected assets by using them to pay commercial creditors to save a company which is not viable and cannot survive. They then have to bankrupt themselves. Follow this rule, and if you have to file an individual bankruptcy, you will still have your nest egg.

63 We will discuss the effect of a judgment and how it becomes an encumbrance or "lien" on the judgment debtor's property in the Chapter on Litigation.

for inadequate consideration can be set aside, both inside and outside of bankruptcy.

Over the last several years, many desperate people have attempted fraudulent or voidable transfers in order to save their property and assets from creditors. These transfers are as simple as the transfer of a spouse's interest in a couple's residence to the other spouse or as complicated as creating multi-tier levels of limited liability companies to hold assets.

Prior to the Great Recession, there were few suits in state court to set aside fraudulent transfers. Generally, these suits were filed by creditors to set aside only the most egregious transfers—and then only in commercial cases. While there have always been more fraudulent transfer suits filed in Bankruptcy Court, these too generally involved more serious and larger transactions.

In recent years, first led by the banks which purchased the assets of failed banks from the FDIC and also by the FDIC's various private equity fund partners who were managing FDIC distressed loan portfolios, and then followed by lots of other lenders, creditors are vigorously pursuing avoidance of alleged fraudulent transfers. Those of us who have defended these cases for many years are finding a new group of litigators and collectors pursuing our clients.

Quite honestly, some of these litigators and the client representatives who are calling the shots have very little idea how difficult a fraudulent transfer case can be to try. For starters, it is extremely difficult to win one of these cases without trying the case. In other words, seldom is summary judgment—or judgment without the necessity of a trial—available to the creditor. This is simply because a fraudulent transfer case is so fact intensive.

Unfortunately, the probability of having a jury trial is a double-edged sword because it is also extremely difficult for the litigating attorneys and the trial judge to explain to the jury the numerous legal and factual issues which are present in even the simplest of fraudulent transfer cases. Of course, if the person sued does not employ a lawyer to provide a defense, the case will be won by the creditor without much difficulty, and the transfer will be avoided.

The lesson is simple. No matter what the facts of the alleged fraudulent transfer are, the debtor and the transferee must obtain competent legal counsel to defend against the suit. Neither the law, nor the facts may be particularly in favor of the defendants, but just the sheer difficulty of the suit may be enough leverage to force a settlement or even result in a win.

Bankruptcy Dischargeability Issues Arising from Fraudulent Transfers

We discussed bankruptcy discharges in the chapter on bankruptcy. If a debtor makes a fraudulent transfer of his or her assets within one year of filing a bankruptcy *with the intent of defrauding creditors*, he or she risks being denied a discharge of *any* of his or her debts. This is a serious problem.

One of my retired law partners[64] who was looking over the original manuscript of this Book reminded me of an old case in which a debtor transferred his one-half interest in his house to his wife for "love and affection," i.e., for no consideration within one year before he filed bankruptcy. The house was mortgaged to the hilt and had no equity. The trustee in bankruptcy filed an objection to discharge based on the fraudulent transfer of the one-half interest within one year of bankruptcy. The defense was that no one was harmed by the transfer. In other words, the defense argued that creditors were no worse off by virtue of the transfer because there was no equity in the house. The court disagreed and barred the debtor's discharge because the debtor *intended* to defraud his creditors in making the transfer of the house to his wife.

---

64 Karen Fagin White, Esquire, and I practiced commercial bankruptcy law and commercial litigation together for over thirty-five years. She is one of the most gifted bankruptcy and creditors' rights lawyers I know.

Summary of Fraudulent and Voidable Transfers Legal Concepts

As you have seen from our discussion above, the concept of most fraudulent or voidable transactions is quite simple. First of all, the asset owner cannot hide or transfer his assets with the intent of hindering or defrauding his creditors. This amounts to an intentional fraud for which even punitive damages may be awarded. Second, an asset owner cannot transfer his or her assets to another person for *no consideration*—in other words by gift—*unless* the asset owner still has enough assets to pay all of his creditors in full, i.e., is still solvent after the transfer. Third, if the asset owner is in business, he/she/it cannot transfer assets out of the business for less than fair consideration if the business will be left with an *unreasonably small capital* base.[65]

---

65 We will see in our later discussion of *alter ego* and *piercing the corporate veil* that using a corporation or LLC as a personal piggy bank is not going to work if it results in the entity not being able to pay its debts.

LITIGATION

I am asked by many financially troubled clients who have been sued by one or more of their creditors, "how long will it be before my creditors will be able to garnish my bank account and take my property?" To properly answer that question, we have to discuss how the litigation system in our country works.

It is very important for you to understand that my discussion below is a generalized discussion. State law and litigation procedures differ from one state to another. If faced with litigation in a particular state, it is important that you employ a licensed lawyer *in that state* to represent you. **Do not rely on my generalized statements.**

Modern litigation in this country usually occurs in the state or federal courts. However, in recent years many litigants have decided to resolve their disputes through use of an out of court process called "alternative dispute resolution" or "ADR." ADR involves either mediation or arbitration or both. We will discuss court litigation first and then get into ADR.

State and Federal Courts

In the United States each state has its own court system with judges and procedures set up by the state's constitution and laws. The state courts handle all state litigation cases including both criminal and civil. In many states, there are various kinds of courts, some of which may handle only certain types of cases. There can be "family courts" which only hear divorce and custody cases and related family issues such as adoptions. Other state courts hear business cases or are limited to hearing civil cases or criminal cases. It simply depends on the state law.

Most cases involving creditor's rights and debtor relief are handled in the state court system, but some are handled in the federal court system.

The United States Constitution establishes a federal court system where federal crimes and certain civil actions are handled. There are numerous books and legal treatises which deal with various aspects of federal civil and criminal procedure and law. As I initially said in the introduction, this Book is not intended to be, nor is it a legal treatise! However, I do want to explain how a creditor's lawsuit against a borrower or debtor can end up in federal court instead of state court.

The U.S. Constitution in Article III, Section 2, provides that the federal court system has jurisdiction to handle civil cases between citizens of different states. This "diversity jurisdiction" was put into the Constitution to protect out of state litigants from what is commonly called "home cooking." When our country was founded, it was perceived that a state court and a state jury might be biased in favor local residents where the suit involved out of sate parties. The remedy was to permit the parties to litigate in the federal court system under "diversity jurisdiction."

Thus, as an example, where the debtor is a resident of Georgia and the creditor is a resident of New York, the New York creditor can sue the Georgia debtor in the federal district court in Georgia where the debtor lives instead of the normal forum (court) which would be the state court where the debtor lives. Congress has established laws providing for this special civil jurisdiction and has restricted it to a minimum amount in dispute of over $75,000.00. Similarly, if an in-state party sues an out of state resident in a state court where the in-state resident lives, the out of state party can "remove" or transfer the case to the federal court so long as the amount in controversy is at least $75,001.00.

In my opinion $75,001.00 minimum is a very low floor for modern commercial litigation. My experience is that federal judges genuinely hate handling commercial collection cases, and Congress should raise the minimum to $500,000 or even more so that most smaller collection cases have to be filed in state court. Unfortunately, I think that the floor amount will only be increased if the banks and big vendors go along with the change. As I have said so many times in this Book, remember that small business and individual borrowers have no lobby in Congress or in their state legislatures.

Moreover, the notion of "home cooking" is really an anachronism in most metropolitan courts, with maybe the exception of courts in rural areas where I can say that I have occasionally experienced or observed some "home cooking," in spite of the fact that I am a born Georgian with a southern accent! Of course, home cooking is always something of great concern when picking a jury at trial. I once was defending a county officer in a suit by one of his out of state creditors which was before a court and jury in his rural county. All three of the judges recused themselves—the chief judge said that my client had taken her to her first high school prom, and that it wouldn't be appropriate for her to sit on the case. The other two judges followed suit. The chief judge brought in a retired judge from another circuit. As we conducted the *voir dire*—the process of picking the jury—it became clear that almost every one of the prospective jurors knew or were related to my client. We finally got twelve individuals, almost all of whom knew my client, but who said that they would not be biased in their decision. The finance company had had enough, and just as I finished by opening statement, they threw in the towel, and agreed to an incredibly low settlement!

Occasionally my clients tell me, "I am a resident of Georgia and the bank I dealt with has a big office here in Georgia. Why are we in federal court? Aren't we both residents of the same state?" The answer is that the bank is a corporation, and it is officially a resident of the state where it was incorporated. So, the bank is probably a resident of Delaware or New

York. Seem fair? Not to me! Federal Court litigation is much more complicated, more expensive and therefore more burdensome on a small business owner than State Court litigation.

Another common pitfall for borrowers is what is called the "venue selection clause" which is common in commercial notes and credit agreements. When included in a contract, a "venue selection clause" requires the parties to the contract to litigate any dispute in the federal or state courts of the state selected by the bank—which is not necessarily where the bank is incorporated or where the loan was made. Let's suppose that the bank is a resident of California, and the borrower lives in Georgia. Is it fair that the Georgia small business has to hire a lawyer in California to defend a suit on the note? Of course not. You might ask, "why would a bank which advertises that it is the borrower's friend and partner file a suit against a borrower in a state where the borrower doesn't live, and which might be hundreds of miles away?" It certainly isn't to make it easy on the borrower! Unfortunately, in commercial cases, the venue selection clauses are usually enforceable unless the borrower has had little or no "contacts" with the state where the bank was incorporated.

That reminds me of another story. I represented a small business in Atlanta which borrowed money from a local bank in Atlanta. The owner of my client had moved from New York to Atlanta several years before and started the business. The bank was headquartered in Birmingham, Alabama, but had a number of offices in Atlanta. Most of their Atlanta customers probably did not know that the bank's home office was in Birmingham. The note went into default, and the bank sued my client in Birmingham. As you can guess, the note had a venue selection clause in it requiring suits to be brought in Birmingham.

Long story short, we were able to defeat the venue selection clause when my client signed an affidavit stating that he had never been to Alabama, nor had he ever dealt with any bankers other than the bankers who were located at the Atlanta bank.

Of course, the effect of venue selection clauses adds tremendous leverage to the lender. The small businessman must now hire a lawyer to represent him or her in the other state. If the case is going to get tried or there are going to be hearings, the principals of the business are going to incur travel expenses and will have to pay to get their witnesses to court. It is no wonder that many small businesspeople just don't respond to the filing of the complaint in the foreign jurisdiction and suffer the entry of a judgment against their company—which is very dangerous.

Ordinarily, a judgment recovered in one state only affects those of the debtor's assets which are located in that state. So, if a Georgia resident is sued in Iowa, the judgment entered either after litigation or by default (if the debtor fails to answer) does not affect his or her assets unless he or she has assets in Iowa. However, any judgment—default or otherwise—can ordinarily be easily "domesticated" through a quick legal process in the business' home state and become just as effective as if it were entered in the home state. Suffice it to say, *The Bank is Not Your Friend!*

How Court Litigation Works

When a small business debtor defaults on a loan, and after the lender has determined that its out-of-court collection efforts have been unsuccessful, it will normally have its lawyer file suit against the borrower and guarantors. Most states have adopted some form of the Federal Rules of Civil Procedure—the written procedures followed by the federal court system. These procedures are followed as the lawsuit progresses. In those states and in the federal judicial system, the official name for the filing made by the creditor is a "**Complaint**." The Complaint, along with a **Summons**, which is a notice, explained below, will be personally served on the business by serving the "registered agent for service" if the business is an incorporated entity and by serving the individual guarantors usually at their residence. All states require an incorporated entity to be listed with whatever state agency handles incorporations. "Service of Process"[66] will either be made by a Sheriff, Marshall, Constable or other state officer or by a private process server.

In the Complaint, the creditor will be called the "Plaintiff," and the debtor or borrower along with the guarantors will be called the "Defendants." The Summons will normally inform the Defendant that an "Answer" or "Motion" must be filed by a certain date, or a judgment will be entered by default. In the federal system, the answer or motion must be filed within 21 days, and in the state systems, it varies and can be as long as 30 to 45 days. **If you or your company are sued, you must employ a lawyer to make sure you timely respond to the Complaint.**

The federal system and some states have adopted rules which attempt to make service of process easier and less expensive. In those jurisdictions, a package containing the Summons and Complaint along with a paper explaining the way the alternative service procedure works is *mailed* to the Defendant rather than served personally. The "carrot" for the Defendant is that if the Defendant signs an acknowledgment of service in which the Defendant waives formal service of process, the length of time to file a motion or answer can be as long as 60 days. I would encourage anyone receiving the alternative service package to sign the acknowledgment and return it in order to gain the extra time. You will need it!

Filing an Answer or Motion

Once a Complaint is filed, the defendant must file a timely answer addressing all of the allegations made by the Plaintiff in the Complaint and also setting forth whatever legal defenses the defendant has. In the federal system and in states which have incorporated the federal rules of civil procedure, the Defendant may alternatively file a motion attacking the

---

66 "Service of Process" is the procedure that the court system requires the Plaintiff to follow in giving legal notice of the filing of the suit to the Defendant. Usually, it involves presenting the summons, complaint and other associated papers in a package to the Defendant or someone of a certain age at his or her residence.

jurisdiction, venue, or whether the lawsuit even states a legal claim against the Defendant. In the federal system and in some, but not all states, the filing of the motion "tolls" or stops the running of the time for filing an answer.[67] The court must then decide the issue argued in the motion before the Defendant is required to file an answer. The motion requires a legal brief—another reason why competent counsel should be employed to represent the Defendant.

While individuals can file answers or motions themselves—they are then called *pro se* litigants—this is a very dangerous practice. In a high percentage of cases the lawsuit will be lost in a very short time because the *pro se* Defendant will not know the procedural rules or have the legal background to analyze what few defenses the Defendant may have to the lawsuit. Also, where the Defendant or one of the Defendants is an entity like a corporation or limited liability company, many states will not allow a non-lawyer owner or officer of the entity to represent the entity in court.

The Road to Judgment

From the bank's (Plaintiff's) perspective, it wants to recover a "judgment" against both the business and the guarantors for the full amount of the indebtedness alleged in its complaint plus interest and attorneys' fees. Once the "road" to judgment has begun with the filing of the Complaint, the Defendant files an Answer responding to the Complaint and/or a motion attacking jurisdiction, venue or whether the Complaint states a claim against the Defendant. Once an Answer is filed, or if a Motion is filed and it does not result in a dismissal of the Complaint, the case proceeds into the "discovery" phase where each party is able to discover facts and evidence which the other side has regarding the issues in the case.

In civil cases the rules and procedures are written so that through discovery each side is theoretically able to learn everything it needs to

---

67 There is no tolling in some states—notably, Georgia—where a timely answer must be filed even if a motion to dismiss is filed. I have always thought this was a legislative trap for out of state lawyers who think the state civil practice act is the exactly the same as in the federal system. Home cooking??

know about the other side's claims or defenses. There are not supposed to be any "Perry Mason" type surprises in civil cases. The procedure for doing this involves one party serving "interrogatories," "requests to produce documents" and other written discovery requests on the other party. "Interrogatories" are written questions directed to a party which the receiving party must answer. Requests to produce documents require the receiving party to produce various categories of documents which are relevant to the case. Under the Federal Rules of Civil Procedure and in other states which have a form of the Federal Rules, there are also "Requests to Admit" certain alleged facts.

Once the written discovery is served and answered[68], the parties may decide to take deposition testimony of the persons having knowledge of various aspects of the case. These will usually be the principals and guarantors of the debt and perhaps the banker or representative of the lender. Most people have never been deposed and have only read or heard about what happens in a deposition. In most states and in the federal system, the deposition is a non-court procedure—i.e., the judge is not present, and the deposition is usually taken in a conference room at one of the lawyers' offices. Years ago in smaller jurisdictions, depositions were often taken at the local courthouse in a conference room or even in the court library. This is still the practice in some areas.

The lawyer "noticing"[69] the deposition will ask the "deponent" questions and the deponent's testimony will be transcribed by a "court reporter" on a stenographic machine so that there is a written transcript of the questions and answers. In larger cases the deposition may even be recorded on video. No matter how it is recorded, it is important to note that the deponent will be put under oath, meaning that he or she must tell the truth. The

---

68 Sometimes, a party may skip or postpone written discovery and begin taking depositions immediately.

69 "Noticing" is a legal term which involves the formal scheduling of a deposition. If the deposition is of a party to the suit, the procedure is usually just to send the notice to his or her lawyer. If the deponent is not a party, then a subpoena may be required.

failure to tell the truth at a deposition can result in criminal proceedings being brought against the deponent for perjury.

Even persons or entities who are not parties can be subject to subpoenas which are issued by the court at the request of the lawyers for the parties and require the person who is served to produce documents and/or be deposed in a deposition.

The scope of civil discovery is established by statute or court rules, depending on the jurisdiction. In the federal system the scope of discovery is set by the Federal Rules of Civil Procedure and generally allows any inquiry which is relevant to a party's claim or defense.

Trial or Summary Judgment

Normally, after the discovery phase of the litigation case, it is time for the judge to determine whether there should be a trial. At this point in the litigation, one or both of the parties may file a motion with the court in which the party asks that the court decide the case without resorting to a trial. In the federal system and in the states which have adopted a form of the Federal Rules of Civil Procedure, the motion is known as a "motion for summary judgment." A motion for summary judgment[70] asks the court to determine whether there are any material facts for a jury or the judge to determine. Remember, it is only the facts which the jury or the judge (in a "bench" trial if there is no jury demanded) decides. The judge always decides all legal issues.

For example, if in the discovery phase of the case, the Defendant-guarantor admits that the money is owed but contends that under the law the guarantee is not enforceable, then it is not necessary for a jury or the judge to determine that factual issue. The judge will only have to determine the legality of the guarantee. On the other hand, if there is a question of fact as to whether the guarantee agreement was actually signed by the

---

70 In some states which do not have a form of the Federal Rules of Civil Procedure, an old-style pleading system is used. The Motion for Summary Judgment may be called Motion for "Non-Suit."

Defendant-guarantor, then that issue would have to be tried by the jury or by the judge in a bench trial.

If there are no material questions of fact, there will be no trial, and the judge will decide whether the Plaintiff is entitled to a judgment or whether judgment should be entered in favor of the Defendant. Conversely, if there are material questions of fact, then a trial will be necessary to determine the factual issues. If a jury trial is demanded by either party, all disputed facts are determined by a jury.[71] If a jury trial is not demanded by a party, then all disputed facts are determined by the judge alone without a jury. As indicated above, this is called a "bench" trial.

Whether a party has the right to a jury trial and whether that right can be waived is a constitutional question which is governed by state or federal law, depending on where the civil action is being tried. In my home state of Georgia, all civil litigants have a right to a trial by jury if they want it. Our Supreme Court has held that a jury trial cannot be waived except after the case is filed. In the federal system, on the other hand, the right to a jury trial can be waived by a contracting party if the waiver is contained in writing. Most bank loan agreements contain jury waivers. Thus, for example, the jury waiver would not be enforceable in a Georgia state court but would be enforceable in a federal court sitting in Georgia.

It has been my experience that most collection cases are never tried, and summary judgment is entered against the Defendant. That said, strategically, the small business owner and guarantors should consider settlement long before the summary judgment stage of the case, thereby eliminating the real possibility of suffering the entry of a judgment.

Small Claims Court

States have established small claims courts for their larger cities and counties to handle small dollar-amount civil disputes. The dollar amount

---

71 A common misunderstanding by lay people is that a jury decides legal questions. That is absolutely not true. A jury only decides disputed facts.

varies from one state to another, but the amount could be anywhere from a few hundred dollars to as much as fifteen to twenty thousand dollars. The procedure in these courts lacks most of the formalities of normal court litigation. In most small claims courts, neither side needs to employ a lawyer, but can if they wish, and filing fees are substantially reduced. In many jurisdictions the Plaintiff can simply fill out a form Complaint in which he or she tells his or her side of the dispute and asks to be awarded a judgment. He or she files the form with the clerk of court, pays the filing fee, and the clerk then sends the Summons and Complaint to the sheriff or other similar court officer to be personally served on the Defendant.

The Defendant may have to file an answer to the Complaint within a specified period of time or may simply have to come to court on the appointed day for the trial and assert his defenses. The whole process is created so that people may resolve their legal disputes quickly and cheaply. Unfortunately, in my state and others, many collection lawyers use the small claims courts for credit card or finance company debts. This results in a decided disadvantage for most Defendants since they are going to appear in the court without a lawyer and are not familiar with trial practice. On the other hand, my observation is that most small claims court judges or magistrates try to do justice and will help the *pro se* (party without a lawyer) Defendant through the trial procedures. Most of the time by law, there is no jury in a small claims court. Again, you need to check your own state law.

Usually, an appeal of a small claims court judgment goes to a civil court of general civil trial jurisdiction rather than the state appellate courts. Some states allow *de novo* ("over again") appeals of the judgments of small claims courts. The rules vary from state to state. If state law allows a *de novo* appeal, then the appeal of the case results in the judgment of the small claims court being set aside, and the case is heard all over again as if the small claims adjudication never happened.

The appealing party (called the "appellant") may be entitled to a jury trial if he or she wants one. However, in some states, if the Defendant does not file an answer and/or does not come to court for the small claims "trial," there is no appeal permitted. This is undoubtedly one of the main reasons why credit card collection lawyers use the small claims courts since they obtain numerous default judgments against unsuspecting consumers.

It makes sense that if you are served with a small claims court Summons and Complaint or if your small business wants to use the small claims court as a Plaintiff, you must familiarize yourself with the procedures prescribed by your state and locality or hire a lawyer to represent you.

Bankruptcy Contested Matters and Adversary Proceedings

In Chapter 3 we discussed bankruptcy law and practice. I decided to wait until this Chapter to discuss lawsuits which are filed in the Bankruptcy Court. These are called "Contested Matters" or "Adversary Proceedings." Bankruptcy Trustees and Debtors can sue third parties (persons not in the bankruptcy proceeding) to avoid "preferences" and "fraudulent transfers," which we discussed in Chapter 5. They can also sue account debtors to collect monies owed to the Debtor or creditors of the Debtor, to set aside void security interests or just to object to the amount of a claim filed by the creditor. These proceedings are handled under a hybrid form of the Federal Rules of Civil Procedure. There is no jury trial, and all trials before the Bankruptcy Judge will be bench trials.

Numerous legal articles and treatises contain discussions dealing with the types of claims which can be litigated in the Bankruptcy Court and how the procedure works for these contested matters and adversary proceedings. The statutory structure of the Bankruptcy Court has a tortured history involving attempts by the Congress to give Bankruptcy Judges more power and the disagreement with these various attempts by the United States Supreme Court. The core problem as stated by the Supreme Court is that only lifetime judges appointed under Article III of the U.S. Constitution can exercise the judicial power of the United States.

A U.S. District Court Judge is an Article III judge. A Bankruptcy Judge is not a lifetime appointee, and is not an Article III Judge, but is said to be an Article I judge.

What has resulted is a somewhat complicated scheme in which the Bankruptcy Court has become part of the United States District Court. The United States District Court through the lifetime appointed United States District Court Judge has full authority and jurisdiction over bankruptcy cases, a fact not appreciated or known by many lawyers and certainly not by most lay people. Thus, the significant limitations on a Bankruptcy Judge's power caused by the Supreme Court's various decisions do not apply to the U.S. District Court Judge who is said to have "plenary" power and jurisdiction.

The District Court delegates the authority to handle bankruptcy cases to the Bankruptcy Judge. Thus, since the Bankruptcy Judge is *not* an Article III lifetime appointed judge, he or she has power and authority which is constitutionally limited. Because of this limited power, the effect of this delegation generally is that some types of litigation in the Bankruptcy Court cannot be decided by the Bankruptcy Judge but must be decided by the District Court Judge unless all of the parties to the dispute agree to be heard by the Bankruptcy Judge. Therefore, constitutionally, there are various defenses which may be available to a litigant who is sued in a Bankruptcy Court.

One piece of advice: because many of the issues which occur in bankruptcy practice involve very complicated legal principals, it is much better, in my opinion, to have the issue tried without a jury before a specialized judge like a Bankruptcy Judge rather than before a generalist district court judge who may have little or no experience in bankruptcy and commercial matters. In fact, although a litigant might have a right to a trial by jury in the District Court, the question is whether a jury would ever be able to understand some of the complexities of bankruptcy related factual issues. This makes it even more imperative that if you are sued in a Bankruptcy Court or have a claim in a bankruptcy case, that you employ competent bankruptcy counsel to help you decide which forum you want to have decide your case. To say the least, bankruptcy practice is very specialized, and your lawyer must be skilled in bankruptcy law.

Confessions of Judgment and Cognovit Notes[72]

A few states allow a party to a promissory note to confess judgment without the need of the lender to file suit if there is a default in the note. Essentially, the party confessing judgment in the note waives the right to a trial and cannot assert any defenses other than the defenses of full payment and lack of signature on the note. The usual provision in a note permits an attorney for the plaintiff (the "cognovit note" holder) to go to the clerk of any court of competent jurisdiction and venue and, on behalf of the Defendant, waive issuance and service of process (i.e., service by a sheriff or process server of a summons and complaint) and confess judgment against the Defendant for whatever amount is due under the note. These statutes generally require that notice be given to the Defendant, usually by the clerk of court *after* the judgment is entered. The Defendant then has a very limited time to object to the judgment on the grounds that the debt has been paid in full or that the Defendant did not sign the note.

The United States Supreme Court in 1972 held that the use of a cognovit note in a commercial transaction involving a corporate defendant and a commercial contractor was constitutional. However, the Court stated that the facts of each case are controlling and suggested that where the contract was very one-sided and there was a great disparity of bargaining power, the waiver of rights might not be effective. Some states, but not all of them that allow confessions of judgment have some safeguards built into the procedure. Thus, in California, an independent attorney must have advised the borrower/customer of the due process rights he or she is giving up.

---

72 Confessions of Judgment are also known as *Cognovit Judgments*. If the Confession of Judgment is found in a promissory note, the note is called a *Cognovit Note*.

Unfortunately, many borrowers and credit customers never read the documentation for the loan or extension of credit. Since a confession of judgment is not something to which a savvy borrower or customer will ever want to agree or permit, if you are a resident of a state which permits confessions of judgment or you are dealing with an out-of-state bank or vendor residing in a state which permits confessions of judgment, you must be very careful to read the note or credit application and make sure that you have stricken through the confession of judgment language.

Don't think that just because your state doesn't allow confessions of judgment that you don't have to worry about them. Suppose that your company buys goods from a vendor in Illinois where confessions of judgment are legal. As part of the credit application, you unknowingly agree to a confession of judgment in the event you fail to pay the vendor's debt. Unfortunately for you, the judgment, once entered in the court in Illinois, can be "domesticated" in your home state and be enforceable just as if it was a suit brought against your company in your home state, and a judgment was entered there against your company. This legal anomaly is the product of what is called the "full faith and credit clause" of the U.S. Constitution which requires each of the states to give full faith and credit to the laws and judgments of each other state.

Finally, courts generally do not like pre-suit confessions of judgment because they deprive the Defendant of due process of law. Many states which permit confessions of judgment limit them to commercial cases and do not enforce them in consumer cases. Also, many courts employ a more stringent scrutiny of the note provisions before entering judgment.

Collecting the Judgment

Once it has a judgment, whether through a bench trial, jury trial or even one entered by a Bankruptcy Court or a small claims court and assuming there is either no appeal or the appeal affirms the granting of the judgment, the creditor (or trustee in the case of a bankruptcy adversary proceeding) may begin its collection actions to enforce the judgment.[73] In most states the obtaining—also called the "recovery"—of a judgment against a debtor, means that the judgment will become a lien or encumbrance on both the personal property and real estate property of the judgment debtor.[74] There may be statutory requirements that the judgment be recorded in the counties or localities where the property is located. Each state has its own laws governing what happens when a judgment is entered against a defendant, and, importantly, how long a creditor can use the judgment to collect from the debtor. For example, in some states, a judgment only lasts for seven or ten years and can't be renewed. In my home state of Georgia, a judgment has to be renewed periodically, but can last forever if properly renewed. My opinion, apparently not shared by the legislators in my home state of Georgia, is that all judgments should be subject to a sunset law. An example of such a law is found in Georgia's smaller neighbor, South Carolina, which limits the effect of a judgment to ten years after which it cannot be renewed and is extinguished.

The creditor's collection activities usually involve what is called "post judgment discovery." The creditor will send interrogatories to the judgment debtor requiring the judgment debtor to disclose where its/his/her assets are located. The creditor may even conduct a deposition of the judgment debtor and probe into what assets the debtor has and where the assets are located. The judgment creditor will use this information to file garnishments of wages—if allowed by state law—garnishments of bank accounts and levy on the judgment debtor's property. Importantly, the information which the debtor is required to produce about his or her financial condition, is *not* required and generally turnover cannot be demanded until *after* a judgment is obtained against the debtor. The debtor's financial condition

---

73 Without getting too technical, in many states a creditor may begin collection efforts even if there is an appeal unless a bond is posted by the judgment defendant to "stay" enforcement of the judgment.

74 But not a lien on property in states which have tenants by the entirety unless both spouses suffer the entry of the judgment.

is generally irrelevant to the issues before the court prior to trial or entry of judgment.

Post judgment discovery is much broader than the pre-judgment discovery we have previously discussed. The limitation on relevancy discussed above is no longer applicable, and the creditor's lawyer may ask any question reasonably calculated to reveal the whereabouts of assets against which the creditor may enforce his or her judgment.

In some states, and in some courts, once a judgment is recovered, there are court rules or statutes that require disclosure by the judgment debtor of his/her/its assets without need for the judgment plaintiff to file any discovery.

Most debtors cannot last financially for very long with a garnishment or other collection actions pending. At this juncture the only solution may be to file bankruptcy. If you are in this situation, please contact a lawyer skilled in commercial law and bankruptcies.

Arbitration and Mediation

Mediation

Arbitration and mediation are misunderstood by many non-lawyer businesspeople. First of all, let's address mediation. Mediation is a form of "alternative dispute resolution"[75] in which both sides of a dispute decide to employ a "mediator" to help them settle the dispute. The mediator may be a lawyer, an active judge or retired judge or someone experienced with the type of dispute. It doesn't have to be a lawyer. Mediation is totally voluntary—unless the contract between the parties requires mediation or a judge orders that the parties to the dispute mediate. **But even if it is required by contract or the judge, there is no obligation for the parties to actually agree to a settlement.**

---

75 As is arbitration which is discussed next.

Mediation has become a "cottage industry" in the last twenty-five years with many "ADR" companies being created which specialize in hosting mediations and arbitrations. Sometimes if a lawsuit has been filed, and the judge orders mediation, the mediation may be conducted by a mediator who works for the court. If so, the mediator generally does not charge for his or her services, or the charge is nominal. Otherwise, the parties—usually the lawyers—pick the mediator, and the parties split the cost. Most mediators charge by the hour, but I have been in mediations where the mediator actually charged by the day.[76]

Here's how mediation works. Usually, the parties and their lawyers meet with the mediator at the mediator's office. If the mediator is part of an ADR company, the company will have a number of conference rooms to accommodate the parties. Otherwise, the mediation may be at one of the lawyer's offices or even in a hotel conference room if the mediator lives out of town.

Prior to the mediation, each side's lawyers will normally prepare a "confidential mediation statement" which will be sent to the mediator, but not served on the other side.[77] These mediation statements usually follow whatever form the mediator directs, but generally, each side tells the facts and legal basis for its position in the dispute. The mediation statements may also tell the strengths and weaknesses of each party's position.

On the day of mediation, the parties and their lawyers will sometimes meet together with the mediator in one of the conference rooms. When this happens the mediator explains to the parties how the mediation

---

76 I was once involved in a mediation of a complicated lawsuit which involved a number of persons and companies, all of which had insurance. The insurance companies were therefore making all of the decisions in the case and paying for the lawyers and other costs. They decided to hire a retired federal judge in Florida to mediate. He charged $10,000 per day and claimed that he mediated 300 days each year. Even if he actually mediated half that amount, he would have earned many times what a federal judge makes in salary! But I suppose the insurance companies were satisfied because after two days, the case settled. Don't worry, mediation in small business cases seldom costs this amount!

77 Some mediators like the mediation statements to be shared with the other side. I do not think that is a good idea because neither side is going to admit its weaknesses in its mediation statement. Confidentially admitting weaknesses is very helpful to the mediator and is a good start of getting the case settled.

will work and asks each of the parties and their lawyers to sign a mediation agreement in which they agree to pay the mediator's fee. The lawyers for each side may give a short opening statement, and then the parties go to separate conference rooms while the mediator does "shuttle diplomacy" between the conference rooms, trying to get each party to settle.

After a number of hours, the parties may arrive at a settlement, or they may not. Generally, the mediator can tell if a settlement is impossible, or if further negotiations will be pointless. If a settlement is agreed to, and depending on how complicated the case is, the mediator may prepare a binding term sheet which will be signed by the parties.[78] The term sheet, in a complicated case, usually just contains the basic terms, and the lawyers will be tasked with drawing up a definitive settlement agreement. Generally, if a dispute arises over the provisions in the definitive agreement, the parties agree as part of the term sheet that the mediator will resolve the dispute.

Most mediators will tell you that they believe the best settlements involve terms that neither party really likes, but the impetus to each party in agreeing to the settlement is to get rid of the litigation, its uncertainty and the costs and time associated with the litigation.

At this point I must tell you a story about some parties who were adamant that they wouldn't settle but agree in any event to participate in mediation. My client was a wealthy older individual who I had represented for years. I also had represented his companies. Unfortunately, he was accused by a female employee of sexual harassment. The facts were very interesting and did not involve any sexual assault or intimacy, but simply involved him saying things to a client in the woman's presence that he thought were complimentary, but were just not acceptable and showed some misogyny on his part. The case was filed in federal court in a state which permitted unlimited damages.

---

78 While just agreeing to mediate does not require a person to settle, *if* the person decides to settle during the conduct of the mediation, then any settlement agreed upon by the parties is said to be "binding."

My client was adamant that he would go to the Supreme Court before "he paid a dime to that woman." The Plaintiff was just as adamant that she was going to make him pay a lot of money. He stressed that he didn't mind paying lawyers' fees—one of the few clients I have ever had who said such a thing! The federal judge ordered that the parties participate in mediation, and it was conducted by a U.S. Magistrate Judge.[79]

The magistrate judge was very good, although my client continued to tell me that going through with the mediation was ridiculous since he did not plan to settle. Finally, having seemingly reached an impasse, the magistrate judge decided to get both sides and the lawyers in a court room and to talk to them together. He positioned the parties in the courtroom so that each side could hear what he would tell the other. Here is how it went.

The magistrate judge went over to the woman and her lawyer and told them that they had a ten percent chance of surviving my client's motion for summary judgment,[80] and that they should consider settling at some reasonable number. He then walked over to where my client and I were sitting across the room and told my client that he had a ninety percent chance of winning on summary judgment—my client smiled broadly. He then told my client that he also had a ten percent chance of not winning on summary judgment and having to try the case before a big city jury which would likely be sympathetic to the victim. The magistrate judge then paused and told my client that he had seen a number of juries "in this city," and he was sure that jurors would not like a rich guy like him, and there was a decent chance that it could award a large sum of money to her. My client immediately saw the light, and we settled for a lot less than it would have cost to try the case.

---

79 U.S. Magistrate Judges are federal judges who are not life-time appointees but are part of every United States District Court. They assist the District Judges in handling parts of civil and criminal litigation and are used by many District Judges to mediate civil cases. If all the Plaintiffs and all of the Defendants agree, the U.S. Magistrate Judge may even serve as the trial judge.

80 Remember from our earlier discussion, this motion requests the court to find that there are no material issues of fact, and that judgment should be entered without trial.

Remember, that mediation is voluntary unless required by contract or by a court. Thus, you may be required or ordered to mediate by a judge, but neither the contract nor the judge can force you to settle!

Arbitration

Arbitration is much different from mediation. Arbitration is basically a form of "private" litigation where the parties litigate their dispute to a conclusion in a non-court forum. It does not involve settlement, although sometimes just as in court litigation, the parties decide to settle during or even prior to the trial. There is a trial (called a "hearing" in arbitration lingo) which is held before an arbitrator[81] instead of a judge. The arbitrator makes the ultimate decision of who wins and who loses. The point of arbitration, just as in court litigation, is for one party to ultimately obtain a judgment against the other party. In an arbitration, the judgment is called an "award," but the award can be, and usually is easily converted to a court judgment through a simple court process. One of the benefits of arbitration is that the whole proceeding is private and not public. The public has no right to attend any of the hearings or view any of the filings made by the parties. In fact, the only part that is public is the arbitration "award," mentioned above, but only if the party winning the arbitration desires to file it with a court and obtain a judgment.

It is extremely important to understand that resolution of a dispute by arbitration instead of litigation must be agreed to by all of the parties to the arbitration. Typically, the agreement to arbitrate is found in a contract between the parties. For example, a contract for the sale of a business might contain a provision which requires all disputes arising from the contract to be arbitrated rather than litigated. Construction contracts, especially those between general contractors and subcontractors, usually require arbitration as do construction contracts between the owner and general

---

81 Some arbitration clauses may require more than one arbitrator. Others may even specify who can serve as an arbitrator. For example, some clauses may specify that at least one of the arbitrators be a certified public accountant.

contractor. Some vendors who extend credit will put an agreement to arbitrate in the fine print in the credit application. Unfortunately, for consumers, many credit card applications have arbitration clauses in them. Finally, for a number of years, some larger banks put arbitration clauses in their promissory notes and credit agreements.[82] Once the parties have agreed contractually to arbitrate their disputes, it is enforceable in court and is binding on the parties. If one party tries to litigate the dispute in court, the court will "stay" the court proceeding and order the parties to arbitration.

Thus, arbitration is always voluntary because there must be a contract signed by both of the parties in which *both* of the parties agree to arbitrate the dispute. Whether each side of a contract *understands* that any dispute *must* be resolved through arbitration is quite another question—even more reason to read every contract and every credit application before you sign! Thus, one party cannot decide to arbitrate without the consent of the other party either in advance or after the dispute arises. There are numerous court cases in which the courts have to decide whether both parties actually gave their consent to binding arbitration because the contractual provisions are not clear as to whether the contractual provision is broad enough to include the issue sought to be arbitrated or to include all of the parties to the dispute.

Binding arbitration in at least some matters is authorized my all states, and on the federal level there is a "Federal Arbitration Act." The state statutes apply in cases where the dispute involves intra-state issues. For example, the state arbitration statute would apply if the parties' contract was entered into within the state, and the parties to the contract are all in-state residents. Contracts which involve interstate commerce are covered by the federal statute. Irrespective of which statute governs the proceeding, many of the state statutes are modeled after the federal statute.

The procedural rules in an arbitration proceeding are often left to the organization which hosts the arbitration. It is quite common to see

---

82 This practice has ceased to be common in recent years, probably because the banks felt that they did not have as much of an upper hand against borrower in arbitrations as they did in straight litigation.

arbitration clauses specify that the arbitration will be held before the American Arbitration Association ("AAA") in accordance with its commercial arbitration rules. Other clauses will allow the party who initiates the arbitration to pick a different host for the arbitration but may require that the AAA commercial rules be used.

The arbitration case is initiated by the filing of an "arbitration demand" with the arbitration host organization. The arbitration demand is very much like a lawsuit complaint and specifies the grounds on which the "claimant" believes entitles it to an award against the "respondent." Depending on the arbitration rules, the respondent then files a response to the demand which is similar to an answer in a lawsuit. At that point the case proceeds in accordance with the rules of the host organization. One or more arbitrators are selected either by agreement of the lawyers or by a procedure established by the host organization.

Once the arbitrator is selected, the lawyers generally meet with the arbitrator to iron out the extent and timing of discovery.[83] There may or may not be depositions and interrogatories. There almost always is a requirement that each side produce documents to the other side which are relevant to the dispute. Once discovery is completed, the arbitrator schedules the "hearing" or trial of the case. In recent years, claimants and respondents have used the procedural vehicle of summary judgment to attempt to have an award granted in their favor without the necessity of a trial. My experience is that arbitrators are more apt to require a hearing rather than to grant summary judgment—another reason why banks changed their minds on requiring arbitration in their notes and credit agreements.

The arbitration hearing is conducted much like a bench trial, i.e., a trial before a judge without a jury. There is no jury in an arbitration. The hearing takes place in an office conference room, although I have actually participated in an arbitration hearing that took place in a hotel conference room. The lawyers present their evidence in the form of testimony and

---

83 In some instances, the arbitration provision in the contract will specify how much discovery is permitted.

documents. There is direct and cross examination of witnesses just as in a lawsuit trial. The entire procedure is much more relaxed than court litigation, and the rules of evidence are not strictly enforced. I have been in cases where the arbitrators told the parties that they would consider any evidence presented whether or not it would have been admitted in a lawsuit trial.[84]

After the conclusion of the case, the arbitrator makes his award. This may happen right after the conclusion, or the arbitrator may take several days or weeks to rule. Depending on what the parties have agreed to, the award may be a simple statement of who won and how much, or it may be in the form of a detailed opinion in which the arbitrator makes findings of fact and conclusions of law—much the same as a judge in a bench trial.

While technically the arbitrator's award may be appealed by filing a motion in court to set it aside, the state and federal statutes make any appeal a very uphill battle. Generally, there has to be proof of some fraudulent conduct, partiality or corruption by the arbitrator or proof that the arbitrator exceeded his power or ruled so "imperfectly" that a final award resolving the dispute was not made. It follows that there are very few appeals of arbitration awards which have been successful. In fact, some courts have now been assessing attorney's fees on litigants who file frivolous appeals of arbitration awards.

To Settle or Not to Settle, That Is the Question

Whatever the type of litigation, at some point the litigants have to decide whether to settle or not. For many borrowers and guarantors, this is a very difficult question. Over many years I have listened to my clients agonize over whether to settle or not. This has convinced me that litigants have great difficulty in looking at a litigation case objectively. I tell every client who is about to engage in litigation the following:

---

84 I once tried an arbitration case before three certified public accountants. During the testimony of one of my first witnesses, my opposing counsel objected to some hearsay testimony, the head arbitrator denied the objection and told the litigants that the three arbitrators were not lawyers or judges and that they intended to hear any evidence which the parties wanted to present to them.

1. The outcome of litigation is unpredictable no matter how sure you are that you will win.

2. Allowing a judge who doesn't know you to decide issues of law that you don't really understand and may never have thought of is risky.

3. But the real risk is allowing your financial well-being or ruination to be determined by a jury of people who are not really your peers, may have nothing in common with you, could be subject to biases against you and really don't want to be involved in the trial in the first place.

The risk is especially worth considering when you consider that you are up against the bank who does not feel sorry for you and doesn't really care if it pushes you into bankruptcy. Remember, *the bank is not your friend.* Instead, the bank is really nothing more than a vault without any feeling.

If you employ competent counsel, this professional can and will look objectively at your case and advise you on your chance of success. Let's suppose that you were sued by the bank, but your commercial litigator has advised you that while your company has no defense, you as a guarantor have a defense because of some mistake in the language used by the bank in the guarantee.[85] You feel that the bank has wronged you. You have used some unkind graphic language in describing the bank and the banker. You believe that "right will triumph over might." **You are wrong!** The civil justice system seldom decides cases on whether one of the litigants is the good guy, and the other is the bad guy. If that were the case, banks and other lenders would seldom win in court!

---

85 This is pretty farfetched. As discussed in the Chapter on Guarantees, the bank's paperwork has been drafted by competent lawyers who seldom make mistakes. If there is a mistake in wording, it will usually be a mistake made by the banker or banker's assistant in filling out the form. On the other hand and as also discussed previously, vendor guarantees, usually contained in the credit application, are much different from bank guarantees, and there is a much greater chance that they will contain mistakes.

The civil justice system relies on rules of evidence and law. Many times, the law results in exactly the opposite occurring. Might wins over right. Juries don't always find in favor of the good guys. Keep this in mind when you consider settlement.

THE SBA AND OTHER GOVERNMENT-RELATED CREDITORS

The Good, Bad and the Ugly[86]

Over my many years of practice, I have represented borrowers who have defaulted on their SBA[87] loans and were being pursued by the lender which made the loan. These borrowers quickly found out that dealing with the SBA lender also involved that lender having to get approvals from a really uncaring governmental agency. They also found out that settlement with the SBA lender was sometimes very difficult.

I also have represented other borrowers who originally owed a local bank which failed and was taken over by the Federal Deposit Insurance Corporation (the "FDIC"). These borrowers soon found out that they now owed the debt to an uncaring and very unsympathetic governmental agency who had the right under federal law to refuse to advance further funds under the loan (if it was open-ended) and could call the loan. As if

---

86 Some borrowers have the unwarranted notion that once a governmental entity like the SBA or the FDIC are on the scene they will help the small business borrower. That is far from the truth. About the only good thing I can say about them is that despite how hard they are to deal with, the loan still works out in a minority of cases.

87 The "SBA is the Small Business Administration, an agency of the U.S. Government.

the bad dream got worse, these failed bank borrowers later found out that the FDIC had sold the loan to a debt buyer who was intent on brutalizing the borrower if that is what it took to collect the indebtedness.[88]

This chapter deals with loans made by the SBA and loans acquired by the FDIC and other government entities, which in some cases, have been assigned to debt buyers.[89]

SBA Loans

Most people who have not had an SBA loan think this is a program which is designed to help small businesses. Some of the people that have borrowed money from SBA lenders may have a different view. I certainly do.

SBA loans are essentially loans to small entrepreneurs, mostly to start up, refinance or expand businesses which cannot get conventional financing or cannot afford their existing debt structure. In fact, there is a requirement in the lengthy SBA application that the borrower "needs" the loan. This translates to "he can't get it anywhere else." According to a fact sheet published by the SBA, the loans range from $25,000 to $5 million. Repayment is generally seven to ten years, although it can be much longer with real estate acquisition or construction loans. The interest rates on SBA loans vary with the amount and length of the loan repayment but are generally pegged to the "prime rate." They absolutely do not offer low interest rates[90], and in some cases, if the borrower could get a loan elsewhere, the rates are more than a local lender would charge.

The SBA loan program provides for loans to be made through qualified banks and lenders or in some cases by direct loans from the government. If the loan is made through a lender, the lender receives anywhere

---

88 As will be discussed later in this Chapter, some of the debt buyers were actually partially owned by the FDIC.

89 During the Great Recession, large companies and equity funds created debt buying entities which purchased literally billions of dollars of defaulted loans. In some cases, these debt buyers paid pennies on the dollar for the loans but were entitled under the law to try to collect the full amount from the borrower and guarantors.

90 The SBA does make low interest disaster loans.

from a fifty to eighty-five percent government guarantee, depending on the particular program and the size of the loan.[91] The guarantee repays the lender the percentage of the loan amount in the event of a default by the borrower. Thus, the lender has a 15 to 50% risk in making the loan. Since the borrowers are high risk, a high percentage of them default after a few years, and the loan goes into some form of collection. I once heard a banker say that the Small Business Administration was in the business of losing money. That is probably not far off from the truth!

So here is some logic: if your business needs a loan, and you have to rely on an SBA guaranteed loan, perhaps your business is not viable or healthy enough to warrant borrowing a lot of money, and since SBA loans suffer a high degree of failure, what are the chances of your success? Should you then pledge all of your company's assets, sign ruinous personal guarantees (along with your spouse or another relative) and perhaps even pledge your residence to secure the loan? Remember that in my practice, I only see the loans which go bad. I am seldom asked to counsel borrowers who can actually pay their loans back! So, take my opinions for what they are worth. Frankly, I can't understand why anyone would want an SBA loan!

As is the case in regular lending, there are fees associated with obtaining an SBA loan. These fees include a fee payable to the SBA for guaranteeing the loan, and possibly other fees charged and collected at closing by the lender. The fees chargeable by the lender are negotiable; the ones charged by the SBA are not. You need to ask up-front what the fees for your particular type of loan are going to be, and importantly, do yourself a favor and shop SBA lenders.

Security for the loan may vary, too. Because default is likely, the SBA likes as much collateral as it can get, and of course, so do the lenders. As one regional SBA manager put it, the SBA wants the borrower to "have skin in the game." But the extent of that "skin" may also be negotiable. If you are purchasing machinery and equipment, you will for sure have to pledge the purchased assets as collateral, and you probably will have to pledge

---

91 A recent SBA "Loan Fact Sheet" states that the maximum SBA guarantee is $3,750,000.

personal assets. Here is where the "rub" is. In addition to the pledge of the company's assets, the SBA requires that anyone with at least a 20 % ownership in the business must sign a personal guarantee of the entire loan. And, it is not unusual for the owner of the business to be asked to pledge his residence as additional collateral—and the fact that the mortgage is likely to be a second or third mortgage doesn't make any difference!

SBA loans are big business, and lots of banks and finance companies have qualified themselves as SBA lenders. You don't have to be a nuclear scientist to figure that these lenders have found a way to make money off of small business entrepreneurs—even if they fail. For example, and this is a little complicated, once the loan is made, the lender can sell off the guaranteed portion of the loan in what is known as the secondary market. The sale is at a premium, and the lender pockets a percentage based on the size of the loan and the percentage covered by the government guarantee. In addition, the lender still receives the interest for the amount of the loan not sold on the secondary market. This is just one example; and there are other ways lenders make money on what is likely to become a bad loan.

Default on an SBA Loan

When the borrower defaults in his or her SBA loan, there is theoretically a way that the borrower can get the SBA to agree to reduce the payments. In practice the SBA lender attempts some dialogue with the borrower and then employs its attorney to continue the collection efforts. The borrower will get a "demand" letter from the lender's attorney, and it is likely that suit will follow. Since there is collateral involved, there is the possibility that the attorney will begin proceedings to repossess the collateral. Worse, the suit will also be against the guarantors of the SBA loan, and if the guarantor's home or other property is collateral, the attorney may begin foreclosure proceedings against the home or other property.

Application in Compromise

At this point, the borrower and the guarantors will have little chance to financially survive without employing a competent attorney with experience in creditors' rights and debtor relief. An attorney may recommend that an "Offer in Compromise" should be formulated and presented to the lender and the SBA. Essentially, an Offer in Compromise is an offer from the borrower to compromise the debt, perhaps making payments over a period of time or even obtaining a partial forgiveness of debt. There are actually two official forms which are used to make an Offer in Compromise, Forms 770 and 1150. Form 770 is a financial statement, and form 1150 is the actual offer of the compromise. Form 770 states that its primary purpose is "for collecting this information (the financial wherewithal of the borrower and guarantors) to evaluate the debtor's financial capacity to repay the debt owed to the Agency and determine to what extent the Agency may compromise the debt, maximize recovery, and protect the interests of the Agency." How nice!

So, what does all of this mean? It means that there are not going to be any "free lunches" for the borrower and guarantors. My observation over many years is the application in compromise will **not** be accepted unless (1) all of the collateral is liquidated (sold), or the value of the collateral is paid to the lender/SBA; (2) any personal collateral of the guarantors is liquidated for the benefit of the lender/SBA, or the guarantors pay the lender/SBA the value of the personal collateral; and (3) the business **and** the guarantors pay as much additional monies to the lender/SBA as their personal financial statements show that they have. Essentially, the business may simply be liquidated and closed down, and the guarantors—unless they are wealthy—will have basically given all of their assets to the lender/SBA. Doesn't sound very good, does it? It suffices to say that neither the lender, nor the SBA is your friend! **Friends don't usually liquidate their friends!**

For those of us who practice bankruptcy law, the above scenario is not that different from what the result would be if the borrower and guarantors filed a Chapter 7 or a Chapter 11 (regular or small business.) The debtor is liquidated or pays its creditors what it owes over time. For the second time, I ask, "why would anyone want to borrow money guaranteed by the SBA?"

Why not just Litigate?

The problem with litigating with the lender/SBA is that in the great majority of cases there are no mistakes in the documentation, and the lender has likely done nothing that would give rise to a lender-liability claim. To make matters worse, if the documentation does have errors, and the errors may mean questionable enforceability *under state law*, the SBA itself may take over the litigation. If that happens some of these state law defenses may no longer be available because federal law now governs collection defenses. The long and short of it is that ultimately the lender or the SBA is going to get a judgment.

Also, during the collection process, the lender will be repossessing and selling its collateral. If the collateral is machinery and equipment, the lender will repossess it and likely sell it for much less than the borrower could get. Whatever pittance the lender receives for the collateral will be credited against the debt. If the collateral includes accounts receivable, the lender may put the accounts "on notification" and directly collect the monies owed from the account debtors. Again, any monies collected is applied against the debt. Under the SBA's liquidation process, the lender must provide the SBA with a litigation plan. The lender reports to the SBA on a monthly basis on the status of each delinquent loan. The lender is also permitted to recover its liquidation expenses.

Once there is a judgment and the collateral is liquidated, the SBA encourages the lender to continue collection efforts before it asks to be paid on the loan guarantee.[92] Once the lender believes that it has collected

---

92 One of the SBA's marketing materials to potential lenders states that, "[A] lender may request payment on the SBA guarantee for loans made under most SBA loan programs after a 60-day uncured delinquency. However, in all loan programs, the SBA encourages lenders to fully liquidate the loan prior to requesting purchase."

as much as it can, the lender requests payment on the SBA guarantee and for reimbursement of its litigation and liquidation expenses.

It Ain't Over til It's Over!

Perhaps the lender determines that the borrower and the guarantors are uncollectible and that the collateral is essentially worthless. This is not a farfetched possibility since the business is likely defunct, and the principals of the borrower who guaranteed the loans are probably insolvent. Let's suppose that the borrower had a service business with little or no hard assets which were pledged to the lender. The lender determines through an appraiser that the cost of repossession and sale is more than would be received at a sale of the collateral. It further determines that the guarantors have been wiped out by the company's demise, and that the third mortgage on the guarantor's home is worthless—i.e., after deducting the amount owed to the first two mortgage holders from the appraised value of the home, there is little or no equity that would benefit the lender. At this point the lender reports to the SBA that it cannot recover anything from the borrower and guarantor and asks that it be paid on the loan guarantee.

The SBA pays off the lender, takes the loan back and charges it off. It then transfers the loan to the U.S. Department of Treasury where it goes into the "Offset" program. This is a fairly esoteric program where the Treasury Department collects the unpaid indebtedness from the guarantors by "offsetting" the guarantors' tax refunds and even, in some cases, taking a percentage of the guarantors' monthly social security checks. Unfortunately, while federal law gives the SBA six years[93] from the borrower's default within which to sue the borrower and guarantors, there is no statute of limitations on the government offsetting tax refunds, social

---

93 The actual statute is 28 U.S.C. § 2415(a), and there is some uncertainty whether the six-year statute begins running at the time of the borrower's default (the better rule) or when the SBA pays off the guarantee.

security and retirement benefits (those that the government owes you as a former government employee).[94]

Strategies for Dealing with a Delinquent SBA Loan

For starters, maybe giving a second thought to even taking out an SBA loan is a good initial strategy. Also, my observation is that many, if not most borrowers do **not** negotiate with the bank or finance company making the SBA loan. In fact, most small business borrowers don't negotiate with any lender from whom they borrow, and of course, they never read the loan documents. Perhaps a good rule to follow is that if you are so eager to take out a large loan, maybe you should slow down, ask yourself why you are in such a hurry and consider that if you can't wait awhile, maybe your business is not viable enough to support it. Remember defaulted loans can lead to the ruination of the business and its owners.

Try not to pledge your personal residence; and as suggested in a prior chapter, try negotiating a cap to the personal guarantees. **Never, never permit your spouse or other family member to guarantee the loan.** Since the SBA, by law, must obtain a personal guarantee from every person owning 20 % of the company, consider (legitimately) reducing the interest of some of your family members. For example, if you and your spouse each own 50 % of the business, but your spouse really has nothing to do with it, consider reducing the spouse's ownership percentage to 19 % or to whatever percentage is below the trigger percentage for the type of SBA loan for which you are applying. Don't be afraid of disclosing what you did to the SBA bank. One thing for sure, you do not ever want to mislead or make a misrepresentation to the SBA. The "penalty of perjury" language in the signature block is for real!

Searching online reveals a number of law firms and other companies who want to help you (for a fee) work out your problems with the bank

---

94 The statute is 31 U.S.C. § 3716. It used to last only ten years, but Congress repealed the limitation in 2008. Maybe Congress is not the small business' friend either!

and the SBA. My guess is that there is little they can do other than to work out some extension of the loan. My suggestion is to try to work out a settlement (compromise) **early** after the default rather than waiting until suit is filed. Neither the bank nor the SBA is generally going to make a better deal after suit, although it is still possible to negotiate a compromise.

If you take nothing from this part of the Chapter dealing with SBA loans, please remember this. The SBA is essentially going to take what it needs from the business and the guarantors to pay the debt in full. That will likely be all of the business' assets. If you are not wealthy—and theoretically if you are, you shouldn't qualify for an SBA loan—then the SBA collection process is going to take all of your non-exempt[95] assets, and it is going to continue theoretically forever. If therefore you are in *extremis* with a defaulted SBA loan, it is probably better to find a competent **commercial** bankruptcy lawyer who can handle either a small business Chapter 11 or a Chapter 7. As I have said numerous times in this Book, it is very important not to wait too long to get advice from a lawyer in the event you are approaching default—whether in an SBA loan or any other loan.

Of course, any good accountant will tell you that you should not overpay federal and state withholding and estimated taxes. Americans, for whatever reason, like to have more money than they owe withheld from their paychecks. They therefore allow the government to hold their money without paying interest until they file their returns at which time, they receive a refund. If you owe on an SBA loan which has been written off, you'll never get the refund. It therefore makes sense to try to match what you are going to owe in taxes with how much you pay. That way, you will be entitled to little or no refund, and the government will at least not have your refund to offset.

---

95 These are assets which under your state law are exempt from collection by a judgment creditor.

The Internal Revenue Service and State Taxing Authorities

The old saying is that "nothing is for sure except death and taxes." Nothing could be truer than when talking about unpaid payroll taxes. Putting income taxes aside, the "lender of last resort" for a small business sometimes is the IRS and the state revenue department. A small business in trouble oftentimes pays other creditors before it pays its payroll taxes. It's the easiest creditor not to pay. The company either doesn't file the payroll tax forms or files them but doesn't pay the IRS the amount due. The same thing happens on the company's state payroll taxes, although they are always much less than the federal taxes. Small business owners think that it is so easy, and it takes the IRS and the state authorities so long to do anything about the non-payment.

This is stupid, dangerous and can create horrendous problems for the small business and its owners. First of all, the IRS and state taxing authorities treat unpaid payroll taxes much differently than they treat unpaid income taxes.[96] Most of payroll taxes are what are called *trust fund taxes*. They are trust fund taxes because the business deducts these taxes from an employee's paycheck, holds them in trust and pays them over to the IRS (or state) when due.

In the federal taxing system, both the employer and the employee pay matching social security and Medicare taxes. The employer's share does **not** constitute trust fund taxes. But the employee's share—that is, the amount of the social security and Medicare taxes which is withheld—are trust fund taxes. Also, the employee's income tax constitutes trust fund taxes since it is withheld from the employees paycheck. The latter is usually the larger amount of the total trust fund taxes except in businesses where most of the employees earn lower wages.[97]

---

96 In fact, those small businesses which are taxed as partnerships like LLC's and S-Corporations, do not pay income tax—all gains and losses are passed down to their owners.

97 Interestingly, even though the payroll taxes are not paid, the employees are not hurt, the IRS and the state taxing authorities treat the taxes as having been paid and permit the employees to show their W-2 income on their individual income tax forms.

Here's an example. Suppose Little Company has two employees, Mary and Jim. They both make the same salary, $1,000 per week. Little Company pays the employer's share of social security and Medicare tax, and Mary and Jim pay federal and state income tax and the employee's share of social security and Medicare tax. So, the company would pay $76.50 per week in social security and Medicare tax and so would both Mary and Jim. However, Mary and Jim would each pay state and federal income tax out of their paycheck. Let's say hypothetically that federal tax would be $250.00 each and the state tax would be $50.00 each.

Little Company would withhold a total of $153.00 from Mary and Jim's paychecks each week for their share of social security and Medicare tax, $500.00 total for their federal income tax and a total of $100.00 for their state income tax. Thus, at each pay period, Little Company would owe the IRS $653.00 in taxes withheld from its two employees and $100.00 to the state for the state income tax plus Little Company's employer's share of social security and Medicare of $153.00. The $653.00 and the $100.00 are the so-called *trust fund taxes*. The employer's share of the social security and Medicare taxes is *not* trust fund tax.

The IRS and the states treat the failure to pay trust fund taxes as a breach of trust. Both federal and state law make certain individuals personally liable for these taxes. These are the so-called "responsible persons," and in the broadest sense, they include the officers, directors, managers and basically anyone who has any company authority over payment of wages and payroll taxes. In the federal system, the personal liability is equal to the principal amount of the trust fund taxes and is called a "100 % penalty." In the state system, it is equal to the state income tax which is withheld from the employee's paycheck.

The federal law governing failure to pay the trust fund payroll taxes and some state laws make an intentional failure to pay a crime. As a retired IRS criminal investigation division agent told me, if the principals of the company are not paying the trust fund taxes so that they can put the monies into their pockets, this is when they risk criminal prosecution. In my practice I seldom see a clear intent by my clients to defraud the government. On the other hand, what I do see are companies who—after being warned, and after being contacted by the IRS or the state revenue authorities—continue to fail to pay payroll taxes. This is a ruinous practice. If you cannot pay wages *and* the taxes due, then you must reduce the wages of your employees to a point where you can pay both, or lay off the employees.

Under federal law, you cannot bankrupt against unpaid trust fund payroll taxes, no matter whether they are state or federal. Under federal law, the IRS has ten years within which to collect these taxes, and after that the government can still use the offset law, explained above, to offset income tax refunds, social security and federal retirement payments. States generally have similar statutes of limitation on how long the state has to collect unpaid taxes.

Assume that the business fails and gets liquidated. All or most of the proceeds of the liquidation goes to the secured bank creditor. Nothing is left to pay the payroll taxes. The IRS and state taxing authorities will assess the owners and other responsible persons for the unpaid principal taxes.[98] Neither the IRS nor the state authorities will usually discount the taxes, but they will permit payment over a period of time. If the amount is very large, then the best remedy is to consider a small business or regular Chapter 11 where there is an automatic extension of time within which to pay the trust fund taxes.

Finally, there are several important strategies to remember when dealing with unpaid payroll taxes. Of course, the first strategy is to always pay them! But if you find that you are delinquent, then the second strategy to follow is to always file the payroll tax returns—even if you can't pay the taxes. If you fail to do so, the IRS (or state) will file them for you, and it is very likely that these returns will show an inflated indebtedness.

---

98 Thankfully, the 100 % penalty assessment in the federal system is only the principal amount of the trust fund taxes and does not include the interest and penalties which are owed by the company. Once the assessment is made, the debt for which the individuals are liable begins to accrue interest.

Secondly, at the time this Book was written, taxpayers still had the right to designate how their payments are applied to a tax debt. Thus, the taxpayer can decide whether a payment should be applied first to trust fund taxes and then to non-trust fund taxes. The business can also decide whether the payment is to be applied against the *principal* tax debt rather than the principal and interest. Previously, designating how a payment is applied was a very easy process because all payments were made by check. Even today, if the business is paying by check, it can annotate any check sent to the IRS or state (if the state allows designation) for delinquent pay-roll taxes with language that it is to be applied to the principal indebtedness owed on trust fund taxes.

IRS Revenue agents do not like designation because they want all payments from the business to be applied against non-trust fund taxes first. They also want payments applied to penalties first, interest second and then to the principal. This makes a lot of sense from the government's point of view because they have the "responsible parties" from which to collect the trust fund taxes if the business goes under. If you are working with a revenue agent, you will have to negotiate how payments are applied as part of your repayment plan.

Unfortunately, the vast number of IRS and state payroll tax payments are made electronically, and there is no way to tell the taxing authority how it is to be applied. Thus, if possible, if you are paying *delinquent* taxes, send the IRS or state a check with the designation clearly described on the check.

The FDIC Bogeyman

I would be remiss if I failed to briefly discuss how the federal government permitted small businesses to be brutalized during and after the Great Recession of 2008-2009. As I write this Chapter, it is only a few months after the new Biden administration took over in Washington. I am hopeful that at some point Congress and the new Administration will review what happened and remedy the mistakes made so that this injustice never happens again. Neither the Obama Administration nor the Trump Administration cared to look at these injustices.

To start off let me discuss an actual case where I represented a small developer—let's call him, Hank. Over the years Hank had some fairly good successes in building or acquiring, leasing, managing and then selling small strip shopping centers and small office buildings in the metropolitan Atlanta, Georgia, area. He would initially obtain the construction or acquisition loans from small local banks rather than the larger banks because they were easier to deal with and were actively looking for developer loans and had fair terms and rates.

Hank entered into a short-term loan with one of these small banks for several million dollars to finance the acquisition and lease-up of a strip shopping center. A part of what was at that time a "garden variety" real estate acquisition loan was an agreement by the bank to advance a certain amount of money to Hank's company to be used for the sole purpose of financing tenant improvements which would be necessary as he leased up the shopping center. Once the shopping center was leased up to a certain percentage, the short-term acquisition loan, including the advances for tenant improvements, would be "taken out" or refinanced with a longer-term permanent loan by another lender. Assuming success, Hank intended to hold and manage the shopping center for a few years and then sell it, making a profit both on the management and the later sale. He had done this successfully a number of times over the years.

Early on in the lease-up phase, Hank received notice that his bank lender had failed and had been taken over by the Federal Deposit Insurance Corporation (the "FDIC"). To make matters worse, he received a letter from the FDIC telling him that under federal law, the FDIC did not have to advance any further funds under the loan contract and that Hank's company was going to have to repay the short term loans which the failed bank had already advanced for the acquisition of the property and the initial tenant improvements.

Hank came to me. I told Hank that as unfair as this seemed, the FDIC was within its rights and that what was contained in the letter was true. This was the beginning of the Great Recession, and credit had totally dried up. Since Hank had not leased-up the shopping center to the percentage necessary to obtain a "take-out" permanent loan, he was stuck with the existing matured loan, now held by the FDIC, and could no longer obtain any loan advances to pay for tenant improvements. Hank tried but was unable to refinance the loan. He then attempted to sell the project to other investors, but they were only willing to pay much less than the amount of the loan. To complicate matters, since Hank did not have the personal capital to finance the tenant improvements necessary to attract tenants, he was unable to lease-up the shopping center so that it would generate cash flow and allow him to propose an installment pay-out of the loan indebtedness.

In the beginning I was dealing with a work-out company which had been hired by the FDIC to deal with borrowers like Hank. Negotiations failed, and eventually Hank received a demand letter from a debt buyer which we later found out had purchased literally billions of dollars of bad loans from the FDIC. The FDIC had acquired these loans from numerous failed banks, one of which was the bank that had made Hank's loan. Research further revealed that the FDIC was a part owner of this debt buyer and that a number of the FDIC/debt buyer partnerships had been formed all over the country. Many of them were started by equity hedge funds, while some, like the one holding Hank's loan, were simply subsidiaries or affiliates of well-known large public companies.

Other debt buyers were larger banks which bought the carcasses of the failed banks at a discount and, incredibly, with a government guarantee on collection of the failed bank's loan portfolio. My experience, and the experience of a number of lawyers specializing in debtor relief was and is that many of these hybrid governmental creditors and successor banks were, and are vicious, and some even "gamed" the system to their advantage and to the detriment of the taxpayers who were footing the losses from the bad loans.

Let's get back to our friend, Hank. Hank's debt buyer began by foreclosing Hank's partially filled shopping center. Under what was then Georgia law, the debt buyer obtained confirmation[99] of the foreclosure in court—we fought hard to show that the debt buyer did not obtain market value at the foreclosure sale, but we lost. Litigation continued in the form of appeals, and finally the debt buyer was able to obtain a large deficiency judgment against Hank who had to file a Chapter 7 bankruptcy.

We found that those debt buyers who were in partnership with the FDIC were, as stated above, brutal, unwilling to settle on reasonable terms, but willing to litigate until the borrower and guarantors were driven into bankruptcy. Even then, some of these debt buyers would attack the bankruptcy guarantors' discharges in bankruptcy, claiming that the borrower or guarantors had given false financial statements to the original bank.

Interestingly, we found that where the debt buyer was another bank, as opposed to an equity fund or FDIC partnership, it was "par for the course" that the successor bank really had no interest in settlement. As we discovered through a lot of research, the reason was simple: the successor bank made more money out of simply periodically writing off portions of the loan and obtaining payment for such write-offs from the FDIC through their arrangement with the FDIC. It made no sense for the successor bank to settle. This is what I mean by gaming the system.

My law partners and I observed numerous similar instances of government sponsored injustice delivered by the very successor banks which had created the crisis but were "bailed out" by the government through so-called "TARP" loans.[100] As a number of my clients asked during the Great Recession, "where is *my* TARP loan?"

One last interesting observation. Our unsuccessful settlement negotiations with several of the successor banks who were gaming the system,

---

99 "Confirmation" was a depression era deficiency protection statute discussed briefly in Chapter 6 in the foreclosure and repossession Chapter of this Book.

100 "TARP" stands for troubled asset relief program which was the government bailout program for troubled banks during the Great Recession.

had an unusual outcome. We had offered reasonable settlements in which the bank would have received hundreds of thousands of dollars, if not millions of dollars over a period of time (including return of their collateral). These settlement proposals were either declined by the successor banks, or in some instances, we never even received a response. Ultimately, the successor bank obtained a judgment against our clients.

What happened then is quite unbelievable. There was silence. After a while, there would be some contact by a collection law firm, and then nothing. Finally, the statute of limitations ran against the judgments, and they were no longer enforceable. We can only guess that at this point the successor bank had totally written off the loan, had been paid in full by the FDIC and was no longer getting paid its' attorneys' fees and costs of collection. It was therefore no longer interested in investing its *own* money into collecting the debt—especially when it had to pay all or a part of the proceeds of collection to the FDIC.

So, who lost? Of course, it was the taxpayers. The FDIC lost money by being gamed by unscrupulous successor banks. But it also was the hundreds of thousands of small businesses and their owners who had to file bankruptcy because of the injustice caused by the FDIC and those entities who purchased the loans and drove them into bankruptcy.

Let's hope that if there is another economic crisis like the Great Recession, Congress and whatever is then the Administration in power will fix the problem and prevent these unscrupulous lenders from brutalizing small businesses and their owners and prevent the successor banks from gaming the system.

CHAPTER 10

THE ANATOMY OF A SMALL BUSINESS WORKOUT

Most of my colleagues in the creditors' rights, debtor-relief area of the law know the so-called four "laws" of what has been called the "commercial jungle." These "laws" summarize how the parties to a small business workout view the process:

1. The borrower or debtor "just needs another million dollars and another thirty days."

2. "Borrowers procrastinate, and lenders are always impatient."

3. "Time is always on the side of the borrower, but never on the side of the lender."

4. "Borrowers are always optimists and lenders are pessimists."

What Is a Commercial Workout?

In a capitalistic society as we have in this country, there are always going to be winners and losers. Most of the businesses that have financial problems are also going to have bank loans, most of which are secured and personally guaranteed. They will also have other creditors such as vendors whose debts are mostly unsecured but may also be personally guaranteed.

What I call a commercial workout is the negotiation of a settlement with the small business' lenders and/or other creditors. The workout may result in a full or partial liquidation, sale or in some cases a refinancing of the debt. There will also have to be some resolution of the principal's personal guarantees. As I have stressed in prior chapters, the sooner a troubled borrower gets competent legal help, the better the chances that the borrower can workout the financial problems with some degree of success.

Tom, a Real Bank Workout Professional

Many years ago, I represented a money-center bank in its small business workouts in the southeastern United States.[101] I had the opportunity to work with a senior Special assets banker in numerous commercial workouts involving millions of dollars of bank loans. We worked together for five years until he retired. He was the best workout professional I have ever met. I learned countless strategies which I use even today. I will call him Tom. Tom had one goal, and that was to maximize the recovery for the bank. That almost never meant driving the debtor into bankruptcy, and it never involved getting emotional or refusing to empathize with an honest troubled debtor. On the other hand, when a troubled debtor crossed or lied to Tom, the guillotine quickly came down on the debtor. Tom could recognize a crook as quickly as anyone I've ever met.

---

101 For this lender at this time, a "small business loan" was anywhere from several million dollars to over $50 million dollars.

Tom knew that understanding a debtor's financial condition and the value of the bank's collateral was a prerequisite to a successful financial workout, and he knew that in almost every case there was a limit to what he could *reasonably* collect from the debtor. Usually, this turned out to be less than the bank was owed. He never employed a strategy of forcing a debtor into agreeing to a workout deal that was impossible for the debtor to perform.

Tom also knew how to use the lawyers that he employed. While he called the shots, he expected me to be his "devil's advocate" and to tell him when I didn't agree with his strategy. He listened to my opinion, and then he made the decision. I seldom disagreed with Tom's approach, but when I did, I told him, and he respected my opinion. Tom was the best of the best, and I have seldom seen a workout or Special Assets banker with anywhere close to the expertise that Tom had.

Unlike with my personal experience working for Tom, my observation of many creditor lawyers is that they simply follow whatever strategies their banker clients devise no matter how flawed.[102] In other words while these lawyers may educate their client representatives on legal issues, they don't counsel their client when they disagree with the strategy. Unfortunately, in a number of cases, the modern-day workout is governed by either inflexible boiler-plate strategies which senior bankers have ordered their worker-bee Special Assets representatives to employ, or they involve stupid strategies dreamed up by inept Special Assets bankers. Sometimes in order to impress the banker, the lawyer finds it necessary to be a hard-ass who will not agree to any reasonable workout.

---

102 One of the things I actually dislike about creditors' lawyers is that they can't do the simplest thing without getting their client's approval. Suppose the debtor's attorney requests a few extra days to respond to a pleading in court. Getting an agreement for a short extension requires the creditor's lawyer to consult with his client. And if the banker has some animosity toward the debtor or the lawyer, the bank's lawyer will deliver an apology to the debtor's lawyer as he tells him that he can't consent. This is total rubbish. I consent to extensions without consulting my client, and I do this when I represent creditors. That is part of my role as a lawyer. It is part of the civility of law practice. If my client doesn't like what I do, he or she can just fire me! By the way, Judges dislike lawyers refusing extensions.

THE BANK IS *NOT* YOUR FRIEND

Often times these flawed strategies result in either ruining the possibility of a decent recovery for the bank through an out-of-court workout, or they drive the debtor into a bankruptcy liquidation where the bank gets little or nothing.

Who Are the Lender's Decision Makers in a Commercial Workout?

As discussed in a prior chapter of this Book, it is common for defaulted loans to be assigned to the Special Assets Department of the bank or lender. At Tom's bank, he and one other individual were the ultimate decision makers in the strategies and in the settlements we made in our workouts. The amount of the loan determined whether Tom could make the decision by himself or whether a colleague needed to sign off on the deal. This procedure has changed over the years, and it is common for the workout banker to report to a supervisor who then must get a committee of senior bankers to approve a workout deal. Unfortunately, what this means is that the small business principal is not really negotiating—and may never negotiate—with the person or persons who can approve a workout deal.

I have had situations arise where we worked long and hard on a deal with the workout banker—who said he would recommend it—only to find that either his supervisor or the committee would not approve it.

Prior to any default in the bank loan, the loan officer who made the loan is the bank's contact with the borrower. Years ago, the loan officer was not only a marketeer who was actively seeking new loans, but he participated in the underwriting of the loan, and incredibly, in the workout of the loan if it went bad. The underwriting process included writing a memorandum explaining how the borrower was financially able to repay the loan, and, importantly, how the bank could get repaid if there was a default. On the basis of the memorandum, the loan officer would make the loan if the amount was within the loan officer's loan approval authority. If it exceeded the amount of the banker's authority, the loan officer's supervisor or a committee of more senior loan officers would have to approve the loan along with the loan officer.

It is important to understand that a bank loan officer's compensation and career is positively affected by the number and amount of *good* loans he or she makes, and negatively affected by the number and amount of his or her loans that go bad. If the loan is a fairly large amount, the loan officer's career can be irreparably damaged. **You can immediately see that there is a conflict of interest and a danger to the bank if the person who made the loan has any significant role in the workout of the loan after there is a default.** The loan officer may have real problems with being objective since he is going to get hurt financially if the bank loses money on the loan. Years ago, banks found out the hard way about allowing the person making the loan to also work out the loan after a default. That is why most savvy lenders have Special Assets Departments.

My experience in recent times is that the loan officer is more of a marketeer than an underwriter and may rely on others to underwrite the loan prior to it being made. The problem for the bank is that the marketeer loan officer may lack the expertise necessary to recognize that a borrower is having financial problems—especially when the loan is current. So, it is not unusual that the bad news is discovered by the loan officer at the time of loan renewal. This could be a number of months after the borrower begins to have financial difficulties, and it may be too late for the bank to recover all of what it is owed.

Let's consider an example of a secured loan made to a borrower to acquire a strip shopping center. The value of income producing property like a strip shopping center is directly related to the amount of the rentals collected from its tenants. Underwriting this kind of loan is difficult because if the borrower has trouble leasing up the center, not only will the value of the center—which is the lender's collateral— be adversely affected, but the ability of the borrower to repay the loan can also be negatively affected because of the reduced tenant revenues. Importantly, the borrower also must have sufficient capital to be able to pay for the tenant improvements necessary to obtain tenants. An experienced loan officer will be monitoring the lease-up of the strip shopping center. If problems occur, the loan officer will put the loan on a "watch list," and involve experienced workout bankers.

I have found over many years that almost all workouts in the small business area have several common phases.

Phase 1 - the Default and Discovery by the Bank

Phase 1 involves a default by the borrower in "covenants" agreed to in the loan documents; or usually worse, the borrower has defaulted in making the required loan payments.

Covenant Defaults

It is common for the credit agreement, and even the promissory note or security documents to contain promises—called covenants—by the borrower to do or not to do certain things concerning the loan. The larger the loan, the more covenants you will find. Some of these covenants are boilerplate. For example, in a secured loan, the borrower will have to promise to keep the bank's collateral insured. Other boiler-plate covenants are that the borrower will only use the proceeds of the loan to fund the operation of the business;[103] and will not permit another creditor to put a lien or other encumbrance on the bank's collateral.

In larger loans, the borrower will typically have to covenant that it will maintain a net worth and collateral values of certain amounts. Depending on the type of loan, a borrower may have to give periodic financial reports to the bank showing that it is in compliance with the financial covenants

---

103 That would not include using the loan proceeds to fund a subsidiary unless the bank agreed in *writing*—not an oral OK by the banker. Do not fall for the "oral OK." Get everything in writing. Bankers get transferred and leave; or worse, they have short memories.

contained in the credit agreement. If the secured loan involves open ended accounts receivable financing,[104] the covenants can be quite involved.

Years ago, if your friendly bank wanted a particular borrower "out of the bank," he or she used covenant defaults to declare the entire loan due and payable and to begin collection efforts. There are numerous cases in the 1980's where overzealous banks and other commercial lenders were sued by their borrowers for treating their borrowers unreasonably when there were covenant defaults. In some cases, the borrower's business was ruined. These lender liability cases resulted in a number of lenders having to pay huge sums of money in damages to the borrowers.[105]

Banks and other commercial lenders in recent times generally work with the borrower to cure the covenant default once it is discovered, assuming it is curable. You will almost always find that depending on the type of covenant default, your loan production banker—the person who made the loan or is handling it—may no longer be involved, and someone from the Special Assets Department of the bank will become your new banker.

As you may expect, some covenant defaults are more serious than others and may be indicators of a possible financial failure of the company. For example, if there is a revenue or net worth covenant, and the borrower dips below these covenants, a savvy lender should investigate what is causing the covenant default and how this affects the ability of the borrower to repay the loan. Is the borrower's business still viable? Is this a temporary problem?

A very serious problem in a loan secured by a security interest in inventory and accounts receivable is the failure to maintain certain

---

104 In this type of secured lending, the lender agrees to loan the borrower a certain total (cap) amount based on the value of the borrower's collateral. The loan is paid back as the accounts receivable are collected. If there is a drop in the value of the collateral, the amount that is available to borrow is reduced. More value equates to more ability to borrow, but never over the cap amount of the loan.

105 A number of these lender liability cases were caused by overzealous bankers who hated their borrower and who were just looking for an excuse to "pull the plug" on the borrower. In one case I heard about from a colleague, the borrower's lawyer discovered a bulls eye target when he was looking through one of the bank's files. The target had the borrower's picture pasted on it, and the picture had dart holes in it!

inventory levels and current amounts of accounts receivable. Thus, if the covenants require that inventory has to be at least $1 million at cost, and there have to be outstanding accounts receivable less than 90 days old of $1 million, a dip in either or both of these values will usually result in the bank requiring the borrower to pay down the loan so that the "collateral coverage ratio" or "CCR"[106] is back to whatever the lender believes is acceptable for the type of loan.

Importantly, while a covenant default may be curable, they often times result in the bank not wanting to continue a banking relationship with the borrower. Bankers sometimes call this a "get out of the bank" default. This can be a real headache for a borrower because the bank may not want to renew the loan or will only renew if the loan is paid down substantially. It therefore is a good rule, that if your business has too many covenant defaults, you should begin looking for another lender—if you can find one.

Payment Defaults

The most serious default is of course a payment default. In a loan which requires periodic payments, missing a payment is a big deal both for the borrower and the lender. Many banks and other lenders have internal policies of how a payment default is treated. Some banks require the loan to be put on a watch list after a certain delinquency period—say, sixty days. When this happens the loan production banker is required to notify other people in the bank that the loan is delinquent. These other people will usually be employed in the Special Assets Department of the bank. At this point the loan production banker—the person you have dealt with—may or may not be further involved with the loan. My experience is that if the loan production banker is still involved, he or she will have no flexibility in

---

106 A CCR of 1.0 means that the collateral is worth the same as the debt. Obviously, few lenders find that acceptable. Generally, depending on the type and mix of collateral, a lender will want something around 1.5 or more. The reason for this is obvious. If the borrower goes into *extremis* or goes out of business, the value of the inventory, accounts and other collateral will shrink dramatically. Thus, the greater the original CCR the better for the lender in a default situation.

dealing with the borrower. All "shots" will be called by the Special Assets bankers.

Before the delinquency period results in a transfer to the Special Assets Department, many times the loan production banker will tell the borrower to do everything the borrower can to **not** go past the "trigger" delinquency date. This is unfortunate since the great majority of payment defaults by a borrower are indicative of some serious financial problem with the business. At that point from the bank's perspective, an experienced workout banker should become involved to protect the bank from loss. Of course, the loan production banker is looking at the default and possible loss to the bank from his or her own perspective because defaults and losses to the bank can be ruinous to his or her banking career.

Special Types of Default

A troubled borrower will generally go to great lengths to keep the bank from calling a default. These involve slowing down or stopping payments to suppliers or other unsecured creditors. We have discussed the usually ruinous action of borrowing from the taxing authorities by not paying payroll taxes. But sometimes actions taken by the borrower can border on, or actually involve violating criminal statutes. For example, in a typical open ended accounts receivable financing arrangement, the borrower will be required to send the bank or lender a periodic "borrowing certificate." The borrower certifies in the "borrowing certificate" that on the date of the certificate, the borrower has accounts receivable under an agreed upon age—like 60 or 90 days—and inventory value of a certain amount at cost. The borrowing certificate contains a formula which has been agreed to in the loan documents. This formula will determine that the borrower has loan "availability" of a certain amount of money based on the amounts certified. This availability is the life blood of the business because that is how much new money the bank will advance to the borrower on that day.

Some borrowers will put incorrect information regarding the amount of inventory and accounts receivable on the borrowing certificate. As an example, suppose the business is in need of a quick advance of $100,000.00. However, the current availability is only $50,000.00 based on the value of inventory and the aged amount of collectible accounts receivable. If the advance rate on inventory is 50 % and the advance rate on accounts receivable is 80 % of those receivables under 90 days old, the business will show additional accounts receivable of $100,000.00 due in 30 days on the borrowing certificate thereby generating another $50,000.00 in availability. The business may do this either by fabricating customer purchases or showing an order not yet filled as an account receivable.[107]

Most lenders treat this dishonest act as the end of the road for the borrower. They will call the loan and begin liquidating their collateral. In extreme cases a bank or other lender will alert the criminal authorities of the borrower's actions because the faxing or emailing of a materially false borrowing certificate constitutes the federal criminal offense of wire fraud.[108] **Do not ever do this!** It is foolhardy to think that you will be able to cover this up. Commercial lenders often audit their borrowers by calling or communicating with its account debtors. They will find it even if it takes several months to do so. Even if your business recovers, and you are able to repay the bank, you can rest assured that this will end your relationship with the bank or lender. What's more, it may be very difficult for you to find another lender. Banks do not deal with dishonest borrowers!

---

107 Generally, the lender's loan agreement will define when an account receivable is eligible for an advance. In most agreements an account is created and is eligible only after the goods are actually shipped to the customer.

108 In the past, before faxes and emails, most savvy lenders would require the borrower to *mail* the borrowing certificate. Hardly any lender would allow the borrower to hand deliver the borrowing certificate to the lender's office. The reason, of course, is that mailing a false borrowing certificate constitutes mail fraud which is part of the wire fraud federal criminal statute. Of course, cheating a bank constitutes the federal criminal defense of bank fraud.

Phase 2 - Meet Your New Banker

If the default—covenant or payment—is not promptly cured, it is likely that the loan will be transferred to the bank's Special Assets Department. That is good and bad news. The good news is that these are the people, subject to the bank's internal policies and procedures, who can make a deal with the borrower and possibly help the borrower stay in business. The bad news is that it is unlikely that the loan will ever be returned to the original loan production banker even if he or she is assisting in the workout. You will now be in what bankers call the "bad bank" as compared with the "good bank" which is where the loan production people, and your original banker works. There are not going to be any more lunches at fancy restaurants!

It is so important for any borrower to understand that when the Special Assets Department becomes involved with your loan, **you need to immediately employ a lawyer with experience in commercial workouts**. Think about it this way: the bank has enormous resources; and it has in-house lawyers and outside lawyers who are generally skilled in creditor's rights law to advise it. Dealing with the bank without counsel is foolhardy and dangerous. If there was ever a time when the title of this Book is true, it is in the workout phase. The bank is looking out for itself, and the only reason it is dealing with you is because at this point, you may be able to help it maximize recovery on the loan.

There are going to be negotiations between the borrower and the bank. The role of the lawyer for the borrower is to advise the borrower as to what rights he has and to help him with devising the correct strategy to follow. The borrower's lawyer can be in the background—which is what I prefer initially—or can actually participate in the negotiations. Remember, though, that a Special Assets Department banker will seldom negotiate alone with the borrower's lawyer. In almost every case, the Special Assets Department banker will have his lawyer participate in any meeting or contact with the borrower's lawyer. Conversely, if the borrower has no lawyer, and the loan is fairly large, you can expect the bank's lawyer to be dealing with the borrower whether he has a lawyer or not. Do not ever negotiate directly with the bank's lawyer or be on a telephone call with the Special Assets banker and his lawyer. Simply politely tell the Special Assets lawyer that you think you need to hire your own lawyer. Ethically, the bank's lawyer must stop speaking with you until you employ your own counsel.[109]

In my experience parties make better deals by negotiating directly with each other than through lawyers. I will say that a number of lawyers disagree with me and will counsel a borrower client or a bank client to always involve lawyers in the negotiations. Again, you should never negotiate with a bank in a meeting or telephone call where the banker's lawyer is present and participating unless you have your own lawyer at the meeting or on the call. However, in my view you should take advantage of a situation where the banker will speak directly with you without having his or her lawyer present. During any conversation with the banker, make sure you say at least once that the purpose of the call or meeting is to try to settle this matter and not let it get out of hand. Using the word, "settle" may prevent the bank from using something you say during the call or meeting against you if you ultimately end up in court.[110] If it is lawful in your state—and it isn't in all states—consider recording the phone call. You might find that the banker is doing exactly that.

Phase 3 - Negotiating a Deal with the Special Assets Banker

There are four suggestions I like to make for clients to follow when they are negotiating with the Special Assets banker. I am presuming that you have a competent lawyer to represent you—whether the lawyer is in the background or out front with the banker and the banker's lawyer. If

---

109 Of course, if you fail to employ counsel, then the Special Assets banker and his lawyer will be back on the phone or in meetings with you—like it or not.

110 Rule 408 of the Federal Rules of Evidence prohibits use of a statement made by either party during settlement negotiations. All states have some version of this rule.

you are negotiating with the banker without legal representation, be very careful. Remember the title of this Book!

The first suggestion is to be a realist. Is your company viable? Most entrepreneurs have great difficulty following this suggestion. They just can't look at their company's financial difficulties in a realistic way. If you have the means to do so, hire a non-lawyer workout specialist to look at your company and give you an objective view of whether it is viable. If the company is not viable, you need to devise a strategy that may include some very hard actions on your part. For example, it may be necessary to liquidate all or a part of the company or even to close down operations. The company may have to file Chapter 11, and you may have to go into bankruptcy. The longer you wait to make this determination, the less likely you will be successful. Do not follow a "pipe dream" hoping that your company will survive, when in fact it has little chance to do so.

My second suggestion applies if you have personally guaranteed the loan and/or have pledged personal assets as collateral—which, frankly, applies to almost everyone I represent! **Devise a strategy which will protect you by maximizing the bank's recovery.** The concept of maximizing the bank's recovery may seem odd, but the more you obtain for the bank, the less you will owe on your personal guarantee. In fact, it may be possible to negotiate a discount on the deficiency you will owe if the bank believes your liquidation or sale of assets will greatly benefit the bank and is far better than the bank can do itself.

If, and only if your company is viable, my third suggestion is that you **devise a strategy to continue the business notwithstanding the bank's actions which appear to prevent it from continuing.** You must first determine whether the business *can* continue. Is the default simply a result of some unforeseen issue that can be resolved—maybe over time? What will it take to resolve the issue? If the bank wants to get rid of you as a customer, is it reasonably possible for you to find another lender offering competitive rates? How long will that take? Can you find other investors?

Recognize that it is always very difficult to find another bank to take out the existing bank where the borrower is having financial difficulties. It may be more feasible to liquidate part of the company's assets and pay down the bank to a point whether it feels more comfortable to continue financing the company for a while longer. Remember, that it is unlikely that the company will ever get out of the Special Assets Department or continue as a regular customer of the bank. The company is going to have to find another lender to stay in business.

We have previously discussed high yield or "hard money" lenders. Unfortunately, this is where many of my clients have gone to obtain what they think are "bridge loans" from the recalcitrant bank to another bank. I have suggested that very few companies can make money, or even survive if they have to pay 25 to 35 percent interest (or more when fees and costs are figured in) on their loans. Don't fall into the high yield lender trap! And don't think that you can use the high yield lender as a "bridge loan" for a few months between the old lender and a new traditional lender. Of course, if your company is not viable, or if borrowing from the high yield lender ruins any viability which was there, there will be no traditional lender who will ever loan any money to you.

Let's presume that you have made a hard decision, and you have come to the conclusion that your company is not going to survive and will have to be liquidated. The bank is likely going to want you to help it liquidate your collateral. As I suggested in the foreclosure chapter of this Book, you can obtain much more for the bank's collateral than the bank can. The bank will collect lots more with you handling the liquidation rather than the bank going through foreclosure and then sale, or in the case of accounts receivable, collecting the accounts receivable without your help. *It bears repeating that this is part of the very little leverage that you have over the bank.*

My fourth suggestion also comes from the foreclosure Chapter and applies if you are going to have to liquidate the bank's collateral. **Try to make a deal with the bank before you liquidate the collateral.** Once you have liquidated the collateral, it is too late. You have lost your leverage. What kind of deal you can make on a deficiency depends, of course, on how much the bank can expect to collect on the liquidation of its collateral. But it also depends on the extent of your guarantee (i.e., is it capped at come amount), the value of any personal assets you pledged and the strength of your personal finances.

The bank is going to want to look at your personal financial statement and will not make a deal on the amount of any deficiency unless you provide it to the bank. Whether and how you do it is somewhat complicated.

Providing Financial Statements to the Bank

When your company borrowed money from the bank, you provided a detailed financial statement of your company to the bank. If you personally guaranteed the loan, the loan production banker asked you for a personal financial statement showing your personal financial situation prior to making the loan. There may be a covenant in the guarantee agreement or in the main credit agreement which requires you to update these financial statements periodically.

If you have made the terrible mistake of giving your personal guarantee to the bank *after* your company defaulted on the loan it is likely that you also gave a personal financial statement to the bank at that time. So, you will not be surprised that in almost every workout I have participated, the lender has asked for additional financial information from my borrower client (i.e., the company) and personal financial statements from the principals who guaranteed the indebtedness. The reason is obvious. Not only does a lender faced with a troubled loan need to know the financial strengths and weaknesses of its borrower, but it also needs to get the same information about the guarantors since they will have to make up the difference between what the company's assets will yield in a liquidation and the amount of the loan.

A personal financial statement (sometimes called a "PFS") is a very important document, not just because it is a prerequisite to obtaining or renewing a loan which has a personal guarantee, but because of the serious harm a *materially false financial statement* can cause a borrower or guarantor. Borrowers and guarantors alike typically exaggerate the values of their assets, and unfortunately fail to list **all** of their assets and **all** of their liabilities. Many times, contingent liabilities are just left off because the borrower or guarantor misunderstands what the phrase, "contingent liabilities," explained below means.

Other times personal debts such as alimony and child support obligations are left off of the PFS. Sometimes the banker realizes that he or she needs a current personal financial statement and asks the customer to prepare one quickly. "Just use the old one and put new numbers by the entries if you need to," he tells the customer. Down the road after a collapse of the company, a lawsuit and bankruptcy, the bank files a discharge case against the guarantor because he neglected to put new liabilities he owed on the revised statement. He didn't do it because he only changed those entries that were *already* on the original form; he didn't add any new entries. Perhaps he didn't think about it.

Let's talk first about the harm that can come to a guarantor where the PFS given to the bank, *prior to the workout or as a part of the workout* is **materially** false. "Materially" is a legal term which means that the incorrect data put on the PFS is more than just "puffing up" values or making inconsequential mistakes. In the context of a false financial statement, it means listing substantial assets which don't really belong to the borrower or guarantor[111] or omitting substantial liabilities. A good way to understand how "materially" works is to ask yourself whether the bank would make the loan or renew it if the incorrect information was not on the PFS or if the PFS correctly listed the information which had been omitted—assuming that the

---

111 One of the first discharge cases I ever tried was against a borrower who had listed a farm on his PFS. Unfortunately, when the truth came out at the trial, he had to admit that he "owned" the farm as a trustee under a trust created by his father for the benefit of the borrower's children, and that he had no beneficial interest in the trust.

bank is relying on the PFS.[112] You will find in the small print on the PFS form which the bank uses—and requires you to use—a statement that in making the loan or offering financial accommodations, the bank will be **relying** on what you put in the PFS. You will generally also find this in the credit agreement or other loan documents. Just saying that it is relying on the PFS is not enough; proof of reliance is required in order to show fraud or to prevent a discharge of the indebtedness from being granted if a bankruptcy is filed.

Providing a bank with an intentionally false financial statement is a federal (and possibly state) crime. If you are unable to settle with the bank and have to file an individual bankruptcy, whether Chapter 7,13 or Chapter 11, a false financial statement can come back to haunt you and result in your not getting a discharge (release) of the indebtedness to the bank. Outside of bankruptcy the bank can sue you for fraud. It therefore goes without saying that intentionally providing the bank with a materially false financial statement is a terrible practice and simply is not worth it!

I have advised clients for many years to explain entries on a personal financial statement. For example, place an asterisk by those assets for which you are just estimating values *and say so*! If you don't know the exact amount of a debt you owe, *say that you don't*. Make sure you show the correct ownership of an asset. Thus, if you own membership interests in an LLC which in turn owns a piece of real estate, make sure you show that you do not own the actual real estate, but instead all or part of the LLC which owns the real estate. Being accurate in stating your income on your PFS may be more difficult than you think because of the different categories of income, e.g., ordinary income, capital gains and losses. One way of handling this is to simply turn over your tax returns to the bank—which probably are going to be requested anyway—and simply show on the PFS under income, "see tax return."

---

112 I had a client who gave a questionable PFS to the bank. The bank sued him not just on his personal guarantee, but the bank also claimed that my client had defrauded the bank by giving it a false PFS. During the discovery phase of the litigation, we found an email from one banker to another saying that the bank was not relying at all on my client's PFS, but instead entirely relying on the company's assets and business.

As I indicated above, many people misunderstand the term, "contingent liabilities." A simplistic definition of "contingent liability" is an obligation for which you are liable but might not ever have to pay. There are actually accounting rules for determining how contingent liabilities figure into one's net worth.[113] Failing to list contingent liabilities is a common mistake which can lead to discharge problems in bankruptcy and other problems outside of bankruptcy such as the refusal of the bank to renew the loan because it thinks the borrower is not being honest.

Now that you have been warned about providing the bank with a false financial statement, the question arises as to when you should give a financial statement to the bank. If you are going to borrow money from the bank, you will have to give the bank a financial statement as part of the application process and update it periodically after the loan is made. However, what if the bank asks for a financial statement *after* you are in default. First of all, let's consider the worst-case scenario. The bank has sued you and is proceeding to repossess its collateral. Unless the bank is genuinely going to agree to a reasonable settlement, what benefit is it to you to provide your personal financial statement to the bank at this stage of its collection efforts? The bank will simply use the PFS to obtain information about your finances to aid it in collecting from you once it gets a judgment against you. So, the answer is no benefit.

Second, let's consider the other extreme. Your company is viable, and if the bank doesn't call the loan, you have a decent chance of working it out. Refusing the bank's request for a financial statement may trigger the bank's calling a default and proceeding to liquidate its collateral. Put a simple way, unless you think you can't trust the bank's intention to work with you, you should consider giving the bank a financial statement.

---

113 Accountants, for example, often determine the percentage probability that some portion of a contingent liability will have to be paid by the guarantor of the debt. Thus, if the guarantee is of a $100,000.00 debt, and because of the strength of the principal debtor and the amount of the collateral pledged, the probability is that the guarantor might have to pay 10% at some time, the accountant would show a $10,000 potential liability on the guarantor's balance sheet.

As we discussed in the Chapter on litigation, once the bank obtains judgment against the borrower and guarantors, the bank has the right to make the borrower and guarantors produce documents and data about their financial condition. This data will include bank account information and descriptions and locations of assets, among other things. This will enable the bank to run garnishments (if allowed by your state) and to collect from the assets disclosed.

This information is *not* required to be turned over until judgment is obtained. Thus, when the bank requests a PFS *prior to entry* of judgment or even institution of suit, it is going to get what would otherwise be *post judgment* discovery. The bottom line is that at this point in the workout, you are providing valuable information to the bank, and you should be getting something for it like a decent chance to work out of the default or settle the deficiency.

One strategy I have used numerous times at this stage of the workout is not to be specific in the location and description of the assets and liabilities on the PFS and not to give the bank a signed PFS. Thus, the PFS can show "cash in banks" of a certain amount, but not disclose the name or location of the bank. An indebtedness can be shown without giving the name of the creditor. Names of limited liability companies and the like do not have to be named, but simply shown. Finally, as I have previously said, signed financial statements, if relied upon by the bank in making accommodations to the borrower and guarantors can be used to oppose a discharge if the borrower and/or guarantors have to file bankruptcy. Suggest that your lawyer give the bank your financial statement with the agreement that if the bank and you settle, you will give the bank a signed more specific financial statement, showing the same net worth (or lack thereof!).

Phase 4 - Settlement and Forbearance

The final phase of a commercial workout involves settlement of the bank's debt—both by the company and the guarantors. Settlement usually consists of one or more of the following: payment of the debt in full or at a discount through some sort of refinancing or capital infusion; liquidation of all or a portion of the bank's collateral which pays off the debt; and a settlement with the guarantors on all or part of any deficiency.

Pre-Negotiation Agreements

During the Great Recession the banks required the borrower and the guarantors to sign a "pre-negotiation" agreement. Essentially the bank was telling the borrower and guarantors that it would not discuss settlement of the debt unless the borrower and guarantors agreed to sign a "pre-negotiation" agreement. While some of the provisions in the pre-negotiation agreement were legitimately intended to prevent misunderstandings and protect the bank, in many cases the pre-negotiation agreement was a trap.

The legitimate part of the pre-negotiation agreement provided that nothing the bankers said in any negotiation session, orally or by email or letter, would be binding on the bank unless it was in a final written agreement signed by the authorized bank officials. A typical pre-negotiation agreement might also state that the bank was under no obligation to settle with the borrowers or guarantors and could withdraw from settlement discussions at any time.

Among the unfair and draconian provisions was an acknowledgment of the liability and amount of the debt and a statement that the borrower and guarantors had no defense on the note and guarantee obligations. This effectively neutralized the ability of the borrower and guarantors to make any defense to liability or amount in the soon-to-come lawsuit. There might also be a waiver or a release by the borrower and guarantor of any lender liability claims the borrower and guarantor might have, even though the factual basis for these claims might not even be known by the borrower and guarantors during this phase of the negotiations.

Pre-Negotiation Agreements which contained this latter type of language are unfair and certainly indicative of the fact that the "*bank is not your friend.*" Be very careful; read the agreement; and employ a lawyer with commercial law experience to help you. I have found that when the bank has required a pre-negotiation letter and the principals of the borrower or their attorney has called the unfair provisions to the bank's attention, most banks will back down. If the bank doesn't back down on the unfair provisions, it is likely that a workout is going to be impossible. So don't sign!

Forbearance Agreement

There are basically two types of Forbearance Agreements. The first type evidences a settlement between the bank and the borrower and guarantors which will generally require certain things like liquidation of collateral and payments to be made over a period of time. The settlement might occur before or after suit is filed or a judgment is entered. Let's call this type of Forbearance Agreement a "Settlement Forbearance Agreement."[114]

The second type is simply an interim step. We'll call this the "Interim Forbearance Agreement." The bank is getting ready to shut the company down or take other serious collection efforts. In this scenario, the bank is agreeing not to go further with enforcing all or some of its rights against the borrower and the guarantors so long as the borrower and guarantors are engaged in activities mandated by the bank. Generally, these activities include liquidation of all or part of the bank's collateral and payment of some sum by the borrower and guarantors. If the borrower and guarantors timely satisfy this Interim Forbearance Agreement, the idea is that the bank might extend the forbearance further.

Suppose that the bank is threatening suit but is negotiating with the borrower and guarantors. The bank may suggest that the borrower and guarantors enter into a Forbearance Agreement in which the bank will promise not to sue or enforce its other remedies (e.g., repossessing or foreclosing collateral) for a stated period of time during which time the borrower will

---

114 If there has not been any litigation or any affirmative collection actions by the bank, the agreement could be just called a Settlement Agreement. However, it likely will have many of the same provisions as I suggest are found in the Settlement Forbearance Agreement.

be obtaining refinancing, sale, or trying to find some other method of paying off the bank—perhaps at a discount. Often times, as time goes on during the forbearance, the borrower will reach a "benchmark" at which time if the borrower has not already paid down the indebtedness to the bank, the borrower will have to liquidate certain assets to do so.

Of course, payment at a discount is a settlement, but payment in full is not. Refinancing and a sale may be just "pipe dreams." Many times, this type of Forbearance Agreement appears to be a faux Settlement Forbearance Agreement, but it really is just a "pipe dream" because refinancing and sale is just not going to happen.

Unfortunately, an Interim Forbearance Agreement usually comes with some bad stuff. The Interim Forbearance Agreement will likely contain nine of the ten provisions listed below for a Settlement Forbearance Agreement. The missing one of the ten will be the release of the borrowers and guarantors. That only happens if there is payment in full or payment of a discounted amount.

For example, I represented a hotel which was having hard times because of the lack of business customers working in the particular area of the country. This created a default in a large loan secured by the hotel property. Both the bank and the owners were hopeful that the problem was only temporary. Accordingly, they entered into an Interim Forbearance Agreement where the installment payments were reduced to the net cash flow of the hotel during every month. Of course, if the net cash flow did not equal the accruing interest, then the indebtedness increased every month. This went on in six months increments for eighteen months. Because the value of the hotel had fallen dramatically because of the lack of guests, our client offered to pay the bank off at a discount by selling the hotel for its market value. The bank declined and ultimately sold the note and mortgage to a bottom feeder, probably for less than we could have gotten it. At that point the Interim Forbearance Agreement terminated. Although the bottom feeder was brutal in how it treated my client, it had gotten such a deal from the bank that it agreed to settle for the fair market value of the hotel—which my client obtained through a quick sale—probably because it was afraid that my client might file Chapter 11.

Each of these forbearance agreements contains one or more "termination events" which provided that the bank's forbearance will end if the borrower or the guarantors engage in certain prohibited conduct. Let's discuss the Settlement Forbearance Agreement in more detail.

The Settlement Forbearance Agreement

Once a settlement is agreed upon and if the settlement of the borrower's indebtedness to the bank is going to take some time, the bank usually requires the borrower and the guarantors to sign a "Forbearance Agreement." Remember this is after there is an agreement to the settlement terms. In fact, the settlement terms are oftentimes set forth in the language of the Forbearance Agreement.

An initial question might be why not just enter into a new credit agreement, note and security agreement. The answer is that the bank wants the usually onerous fine print—which includes covenants and other provisions—of the original agreements to remain in force *as only modified by the Forbearance Agreement* and it does not want there to be any question about the *priority* of its security interest in the borrower's assets. There is also the possible issue that a Bankruptcy Court might determine that payments made pursuant to the new documents might constitute "preferences" which could be set aside.

As we have said, the essence of the Settlement Forbearance Agreement is that the bank will not enforce its default remedies (e.g., repossession, foreclosure, etc.) so long as the borrower and guarantors are current in their settlement obligations as set forth in the Forbearance Agreement. You can expect the draft of the Forbearance Agreement proposed by the bank to be totally one-sided. As I have suggested many times in this Book, you need to employ an attorney who has experience in commercial law and commercial workouts to represent you in negotiating the Forbearance Agreement.

The usual one-sided Settlement Forbearance Agreement will be between the bank on the one hand and the borrower and guarantors on the other hand and will contain most, if not all of the following provisions:

1. An admission by the borrower and guarantors that the debt is owing with no defenses or offsets.

2. A release of all claims which the borrower and the guarantors have against the bank as of the date of the Forbearance Agreement. This release will be extremely broad and will be effective even if the borrower and guarantors default in the settlement terms. It will also "abrogate"[115] any lender liability claims which the borrower and guarantors may have.

3. An agreement by the borrower and guarantors to satisfy all of the terms of the settlement. And, the bank means *all!*

4. A complete statement of the settlement terms, including the dates by which certain events such as liquidation of certain of the collateral must occur and when payments by the borrower and guarantors are due and payable. There may be a "grace" period for late payments.

5. An agreement by the bank that so long as the borrower and guarantors are not in default on the terms of the settlement, the bank will not enforce its rights against the borrower and guarantors.

---

115 "Abrogate" is a word which lawyers like to use which means negate, nullify, annul, etc. I threw that in just to keep you on your toes!

6. A list of defaults, which importantly will provide that a default under the original loan agreements—*except if no longer effective because a particular default was modified or deleted by the Forbearance Agreement*—will result in early termination of the Forbearance Agreement. This is a very dangerous provision and will be discussed in detail below.

7. A statement of when the Forbearance Agreement will terminate in the event of a default by the borrower and guarantors.

8. A statement of what happens if the Forbearance Agreement terminates earlier because of default, i.e., what remedies the bank will have in such event.

9. A "spring back" provision which negates any agreement by the bank to discount the indebtedness as part of the settlement. This provision provides that in the event the Forbearance Agreement terminates early because of a default, the indebtedness owed by the borrower and guarantors will go back to the original indebtedness, including all accrued interest, late charges and attorneys' fees, less whatever the bank has received in liquidation proceeds and payments. In other words, after a default, the borrower and guarantors don't get the benefit of any discount.

10. A complete release of the borrower and guarantors after receipt of payment in full or payment of the agreed upon discounted amount.

Item 6 above is a very "red herring." In many cases this is boiler-plate language, but in other cases it is intentionally put in the Forbearance Agreement in order to snooker the borrowers and guarantors. The problem with this provision is that many of the covenants and warranties no longer can apply even if they are not expressly eliminated by the Forbearance

Agreement. For example, at this point in the workout, there may be a judgment against the borrower (and guarantors), or the company has stopped operating. It is likely insolvent (legal and equitably)—which violates a boilerplate covenant in most credit agreements. Since it is not operating or its operations have been reduced dramatically, it will be impossible to meet any covenants which require a certain amount of revenues.

How do you address this in the Forbearance Agreement? I like to state in the Forbearance Agreement that, "all covenants and warranties in the loan documents are no longer effective except _____." This then lets you and the bank decide which covenants and warranties are really relevant (and possible) in the Forbearance Agreement. Never, never agree to covenants and warranties which are impossible to perform. It will give the bank a way out of the Forbearance Agreement.

The Consent Order or Consent Judgment

When the bank is in litigation with the borrower and guarantors, it may be that a discounted debt agreement can be entered into. Having already had to sue the borrower and guarantors, the bank is unlikely to want to just dismiss the lawsuit and enter into a Settlement Forbearance Agreement because if there is a default in the agreement, the bank will have to go to the expense of filing another lawsuit.[116] Most banks will insist on a consent judgment and the execution of a Forbearance Agreement by the parties.

In some instances, depending on what state you are in and also whether the court will go along with payment terms stretching out over a number of years, the court may enter a "consent order" rather than a "consent judgment." The consent order is quite similar to a confession of judgment except that it is entered *after* the litigation is instituted. The consent order sets out the terms of the settlement and provides that if there is

---

116 I am <u>not</u> suggesting that you shouldn't ask for a dismissal. I have represented clients in litigation where the bank did exactly that. However, the debtor was required to secure what was otherwise an unsecured debt.

a default the lender's attorney may file an affidavit detailing the default and obtain a judgment against the borrower and guarantors for the full amount sued for, less actual payments. From the court's perspective, the court will simply administratively close the case pending either its activation if there is a default or its dismissal with prejudice if all payments are made. The consent order is obviously preferable to the consent judgment since the former does not constitute a lien or encumbrance on the assets of the borrower or guarantors.

Threats of Bankruptcy

Many attorneys for borrowers and guarantors like to threaten the bank with the filing of some sort of bankruptcy case, i.e., Chapter 7, Chapter 11 or in the case of a consumer or small proprietorship, a Chapter 13. The idea, they think, is to gain a degree of leverage over the bank to force a better result in a workout. **I hate to say it, but it seldom works;** and when it does work, it is usually because the banker and/or the banker's lawyer is inept or doesn't know enough commercial and bankruptcy law to analyze whether the debtor's bankruptcy would actually benefit the bank. On the other hand, there are some cases where a bankruptcy would be bad for the bank. In such a case, the threat might just create some leverage for the debtor.

It has always been my practice—something my mentors taught me when I first started practicing in this area of the law—never to threaten bankruptcy for a debtor client unless my client was prepared to file if the threat did not work. Because of this practice, other lawyers in my legal community know that when I threaten bankruptcy, I mean it!

After many years of representing creditors, I can tell you that most times bankruptcy will either actually benefit the bank or will not harm it. Let's examine some *good, bad and ugly* scenarios.

1. The bank's collateral is worth the debt if liquidated in an orderly way. Bankruptcy will allow the liquidation to occur under Bankruptcy Court supervision. ***Bankruptcy filing is probably good for the bank!***

2. The debtor has lots of unsecured creditors, many of whom are filing suit against the debtor. Perhaps some have already obtained judgments. In my area of practice, we say that the debtor is being subjected to the *rule of grab*. It is almost impossible for a business to operate in this environment. It is also impossible for the business to enter into a successful workout with the bank. ***Bankruptcy filing is good for the bank!***

3. The value of the bank's collateral is low even if liquidated in an orderly fashion. Accordingly, the bank is really an unsecured creditor. Taking payments from the debtor may be avoided as preferences under bankruptcy law if there is a filing. A quick filing may permit the bank to share in the proceeds available to unsecured creditors in a bankruptcy liquidation or reorganization of the debtor. On the other hand, any payments made by the debtor to the bank within ninety days before the filing could be avoided and clawed back by a trustee or debtor-in-possession. ***Bankruptcy filing may be good or bad, depending on the circumstances!***

4. During the workout the bank has obtained additional collateral from the debtor or has recovered a judgment against the debtor which, under state law, has become a lien on the property of the debtor. The debtor threatens to file bankruptcy, and ninety days has not passed since the additional collateral was obtained or the

judgment was recovered. ***Bankruptcy filing would definitely be bad for the bank!***[117]

5. Finally, and we don't see much of this anymore, the bank has been guilty of some type of egregious conduct which has injured the borrower and guarantors. In other words, the bank has engaged in conduct which would be actionable by the debtor *or* its creditors. Perhaps the bank is able to bully the debtor as long as it is out of bankruptcy, and the bank can control the money flow to the debtor's lawyers and prevent them from suing the bank. If this is real—and remember, the bank has a bevy of lawyers, some of whom undoubtedly are knowledgeable enough to know whether the bank has exposure for lender liability—the bank will not be interested in the debtor filing bankruptcy.[118] ***Bankruptcy filing is definitely not good for the bank!***

Special Workout Situations Involving Contractors

Many small businesses are involved in the construction industry. As we have seen, the Uniform Commercial Code enacted in almost all of the states is quite similar. **This is not the case with the law governing construction disputes.** Construction law differs from one state to another. Accordingly, it is really important to seek the advice of an attorney skilled in construction law in your state.

---

117 In this scenario, the additional collateral and the judgment lien would be preferential transfers and would be avoidable under the bankruptcy law. As explained in the chapter on bankruptcy, a preference can be a payment or a transfer of property or the obtaining of a lien or security interest in property of the debtor.

118 As discussed elsewhere in this Book, "Lender Liability" became a cottage industry for debtor's lawyers in the 1980's because of incredibly stupid actions by numerous banks and other lenders. There were enormous judgments recovered against some large lenders. Then lenders got smart, and lender liability cases disappeared.

Special issues arise during workouts between banks and contractors in the construction industry. In my view the issues arise because the Special Assets bankers handling the workout do not understand how construction contracts and sureties work. Many times, the banker's lack of knowledge results in the bank shutting down the contractor and discovering to its dismay that its accounts receivable collateral is totally worthless or belongs to the surety.

Construction Law and Practice Primer

General contractors essentially render services to the owner of the construction project, consisting of supervising and hiring subcontractors to build the project and in some cases suppliers to supply the construction materials[119]. They are paid for their services by the owner and in turn pay their subcontractors and suppliers. The general contractor may borrow money from a bank and pledge its construction accounts receivable as collateral. As any general contractor or subcontractor will tell you, because of the nature of the construction business, collection of accounts receivable is always an issue. There is almost always "retainage" or monies withheld by the owner or general contractor until the project is finished and all construction issues are satisfied to the owner or general contractor's satisfaction. Sometimes, there is a dispute between the owner and the general contractor or the general contractor and a subcontractor. Payment may be withheld until the dispute is resolved, and that may involve litigation and often times arbitration. The contract may contain a "pay when paid" provision, which if enforced in your state,[120] will delay payment to a subcontractor or supplier until the general contractor is paid.

---

119 Construction materials are also supplied by subcontractors who contract with the suppliers.

120 Georgia enforces this provision, but other states do not enforce it or only enforce the provision for a "reasonable time." You must check with a construction law attorney in your state if that becomes an issue.

Sureties

Many construction projects are bonded. This adds an additional very powerful party to the participants in the construction project. Thus, a general contractor will likely have to post a bond with the owner, and a subcontractor may have to post a bond with the general contractor. These bonds are either "performance" bonds or "payment" bonds. These are explained below.

There are numerous insurance companies which write these bonds. When they do, they are known as "sureties." Many small contractors and subcontractors do not truly understand how surety law works, nor do they ever read the surety contract between the surety and the owner/general contractor or the indemnity agreement which the contractor or subcontractor *and their owners* have to sign in favor of the surety.

There are several agreements which govern the bonding arrangement. The performance bond is the surety's agreement to stand behind the contractor/subcontractor and finish its obligations under the construction contract if there is a default. If the contractor or sub-contractor has financial difficulties and cannot finish the job, the surety takes over the contract, finishes it and, pursuant to the terms of the indemnity agreement explained below, charges the contractor/subcontractor with the loss the surety suffers. This can result in financial ruin for the defaulting contractor or subcontractor.

The indemnity agreement is the agreement between the contractor/subcontractor and the surety, and most of the time also with the owners of the contractor/subcontractor. The indemnity agreement provides that the contractor/subcontractor and the owners of the contractor/subcontractor will "indemnify" or agree to pay the surety for any losses, including attorneys' fees and other costs, incurred by the surety if it is called upon to finish the job or correct any deficiencies. It likewise can be financially ruinous for the contractor/subcontractor and its owners.

Payment bonds are similar, except that they usually are posted by the general contractor and cover the owner in the event the general contractor fails to pay its subcontractors and suppliers as required by its construction contract with the owner. There is always an indemnity agreement between the general contractor and its principals with the surety to cover the surety's losses.

When the owner declares a default and calls upon the bonding company, the bonding company is entitled by law to be paid by the owner the part of the contract price which has not been paid to the general contractor who defaulted. The same thing applies when a general contractor declares that a subcontractor is in default, and the subcontractor has posted a bond. Importantly, the bonding company is entitled to this account receivable ordinarily payable to the general contractor (or subcontractor) *even if it has been pledged*[121] *along with other accounts receivable to the general contractor's (or sub-contractor's) bank as collateral.* What this means is that the bank's security interest in this account receivable is worthless.

The same thing occurs when a general contractor doesn't pay it subcontractors and suppliers, and they file liens against the owner's property. The owner is entitled under the law to offset whatever sums that are required to satisfy the lien claims against whatever the general contractor is owned. That, in turn, reduces the amount of money the owner owes the general contractor.

Effect on a Financial Workout

If the general contractor or subcontractor depends on the bank's continuing financing of its operation through an open-ended credit facility, or if the general contractor is unable to pay the installments due under a secured fixed loan, how the bank works out the default will likely

---

121 "Pledged" means that the general contractor grants to a lender a security interest in its accounts receivable.

determine whether the bank recovers any significant amount of its loan. Here is an example:

Suppose the general contractor under-quotes a substantial job. It begins losing money, and the losses cause it to default on its secured loan with the bank. If the job is bonded, and the bank "pulls the plug" on the general contractor, the surety will take over the project, and the bank's collateral will be worthless. On the other hand, if a savvy Special Assets banker understands how the construction industry works, the banker will analyze the situation and determine whether the general contractor is viable enough to continue operations so that it finishes the contract, and the account receivable is salvaged. The Special assets banker may have to "pick and choose" which construction contracts the general contractor is able to finish, but if the banker handles the credit properly, the bank will collect a substantial portion of its loan, and possibly the contractor will survive. The scary decision which the Special Assets banker may have to make will be whether the bank may have to actually advance new money to the general contractor to keep it in business and able to finish its construction projects.

It is easy to see that a contractor workout is very difficult with a lot of pitfalls along the way. My experience is that few Special Asset bankers know how to work out a construction industry debt. In one instance in which I am very familiar, the bank shut down a viable contractor who owed it $6 million. After the surety took over numerous jobs and numerous liens were filed on multiple projects, a major part of the bank's accounts receivable collateral dried up, and it ultimately recovered only $2 million. Not only was *the bank not the friend of this contractor*, but it's mismanagement of the credit facility, resulted in the bankruptcy liquidation of the contractor and substantial losses to the bank.

The same type of scenario occurs when the bank finances a subcontractor or supplier. In one case in which I represented the subcontractor, the general contractor and the owner had a dispute, and the owner refused to pay the general contractor. Because of the "pay when paid" provision in the sub-contract, my client was not paid, and he defaulted on a number of his contracts with his suppliers and on his debt to the bank. The bank sued, but quickly found out that all of its accounts receivable collateral was worthless because of lien claims made by the suppliers. The subcontractor went out of business, and its owner had to file bankruptcy. The bank lost the entire amount of the loan.

I have always wondered why a bank would ever loan money to a contractor if the main collateral was the contractor's construction accounts receivable. I think the answer is that the loan production banker, i.e., the banker who makes the loan, is probably not experienced in the construction industry, doesn't understand how the industry works or its pitfalls, and he is also a marketeer who wants to put as many loans on the bank's books as possible irrespective of the risk.

Notwithstanding the ineptness of the marketeer, you would at least think that the loan underwriting committee would have members who were experienced enough to recognize the risk of making such loans. That is not to say that I am against banks making loans to contractors, generals or subs. To the contrary, I think that a prudent banker and a prudent contractor can structure a loan which *has a chance to work for both*.

CHAPTER 11 BANKRUPTCY

Introduction

If negotiations with the bank fail, **the last resort**—and I stress it is the last resort—is to consider filing bankruptcy. We have previously discussed Chapter 7 which is the liquidation chapter of the Bankruptcy Code, mostly used by consumer debtors.[122] However, Chapter 11 may be a possible remedy if all else fails, and *there is a reasonable possibility* that all or some part of the company can be saved and reorganized or sold or liquidated. In a Chapter 11, the management of the debtor company usually remains in place—it's called the "debtor-in-possession" or "DIP," and it continues to operate the business during the Chapter 11.

If liquidation is the only reasonable course, Chapter 11 can also be used where an orderly liquidation would benefit the debtor and its creditors, and the management of the debtor is best suited to conduct the liquidation. For example, a Chapter 11 liquidation might be used to pay

---

122 As I have said in the bankruptcy chapter, the general rule is *not* to file a Chapter 7 for an entity like an LLC or corporation. You will never use the entity again or shouldn't. We discussed in the bankruptcy chapter that there are a few legitimate reasons to file a Chapter 7 for an entity. For example, a Chapter 7 might be of benefit if the company owes payroll taxes for which the principals will become liable *and* there is equity in the assets over and above any secured debt which could be used to pay all or part of the taxes. However, in a Chapter 7, unlike in most Chapter 11 cases, a Trustee will be doing the liquidation rather than the debtor-in-possession.

off a secured creditor, reduce the financial exposure for guarantors of the secured loan and to pay off delinquent taxes. In a Chapter 11 liquidation, as in the Chapter 11 reorganization the management of the debtor company generally remains in place as the DIP and conducts the liquidation.[123]

Before I will file a Chapter 11 for any client, I always advise the client of the risk of filing. Chapter 11 is in most cases a one-way street much like in the song, *Hotel California*, "you can check-out any time, but you can never leave." Realistically, the one-way street either leads to some success or it leads to liquidation, possibly resulting in the DIP "checking-out," and being replaced by a trustee. Thus, unless a settlement is made with creditors during the Chapter 11, the case will not be dismissed, but will continue until the creditors and debtor agree to a feasible plan which can be confirmed (explained below) or to a liquidation. In short it is foolhardy to think that if a Chapter 11 filing does not work, the case can easily be dismissed. Chapter 11 is not a "try it and see if you like it" remedy.

Moreover, filing a Chapter 11, puts all of the good, bad and ugly conduct of the management of a debtor on the table for all of the creditors, the United States Trustee and the Bankruptcy Court to look at, analyze and possibly to take action against management and the owners. Small business owners, and in fact owners of some large businesses do things that may really be of little consequence as long as the business is paying its bills and is solvent. When it gets into financial difficulties, these actions can lead to serious problems for the owners. Thus, bankruptcy exacerbates any problems associated with the pre-bankruptcy actions by management and owners.

If there has been any criminal conduct by any of the principals of the debtor, you can expect that the criminal authorities will be alerted once the case is filed, and it is likely that a Trustee will be appointed.

---

123 Where there has been mismanagement or fraudulent conduct by the existing management, the bankruptcy court may order that a Trustee be appointed to manage the company. Although the Trustee can file a plan of reorganization or sell the company, in most instances, the Trustee liquidates it.

A Chapter 11 Primer

Chapter 11 of the Bankruptcy Code is derived from Chapters X and XI[124] of the Bankruptcy Act of 1898. Chapter X was an extremely complicated reorganization proceeding only available to corporations, and Chapter XI of the Act was available to individuals and corporations but only permitted modification of unsecured debt. The current Chapter 11 is essentially a combination of the two, is still complicated, expensive and can be lengthy. Under the Bankruptcy Code, persons and businesses[125] are eligible to file Chapter 11 cases.

The debtor remains in possession of the debtor's assets and operates its business and, as stated above, is called the "Debtor in Possession" or "DIP." Under certain circumstances where there is fraud or gross mismanagement, the Bankruptcy Court may order that the United States Trustee appoint a Trustee. Once a Trustee is appointed by the United States Trustee, the debtor loses control of the business to the Trustee who will determine whether continuing in Chapter 11 is warranted or whether the case should be converted to Chapter 7. The Trustee may continue the Chapter 11 case and file a plan which reorganizes or liquidates the company.[126]

In larger Chapter 11 cases, an "Unsecured Creditors' Committee," usually made up of a representative from each of the larger unsecured creditors, is appointed by the United States Trustee. The Committee's function is to protect the rights of the unsecured creditors, and it may employ attorneys to represent it. The attorneys are paid out of the bankruptcy estate, i.e., by the Debtor in Possession. In even larger, more complicated Chapter 11 cases, there can be other committees appointed by the United States Trustee. Thus, in a large case, there can be one or more bondholders

---

124 Note the roman numerals. The later Bankruptcy Code did away with the roman numerals and replaced them with normal Arabic numbers.

125 Insurance companies, banks and certain other similar types of entities are not eligible to file bankruptcy.

126 Liquidation can involve sale of all or a portion of the company to a buyer, or a sale of its assets to several buyers.

committees or even an equity security holders (shareholders) committee if it appears that the debtor is solvent. You can see how a Chapter 11 case can get very expensive!

The Chapter 11 Plan

At a certain point in the Chapter 11 proceeding, the Debtor will file a "Plan" in which it proposes a methodology for paying its secured, priority[127] and unsecured and creditors. For example, in a reorganization case the debtor may propose to stretch out payment of its indebtedness to secured creditors; or it may decide to actually surrender all or a portion of the secured creditor's collateral, and to pay any deficiency owed to the secured creditor in the same way it proposes in the plan to pay unsecured creditors. The Plan may stretch out payments to taxing authorities which is automatically permitted under a provision of the Bankruptcy Code.

One of the most advantageous provisions of Chapter 11, is the ability to "reject" burdensome leases. This means that the debtor can get out of a real estate lease no matter how many months or years are left. But there's more. The Bankruptcy Code significantly *limits* the amount of damages which the real estate lessor can claim against the debtor, and which must be handled through the Chapter 11 plan. Thus, even though there are many years left on a lease, the lessor's claim for damages is limited to a relatively small percent of these damages. This is especially helpful where the debtor has a number of locations and needs to close the unprofitable ones.

As I have said, the Plan may be one of reorganization or liquidation and is sent to creditors along with a "Disclosure Statement." The Disclosure Statement is similar to a securities prospectus and must be approved by the

---

127 The Bankruptcy Code contains a sequential list of certain categories of "priority" creditors. Each category in the list must be paid in full before the next one on the list gets paid. The list contains alimony and child support (in an individual case), expenses of administration, unpaid wages to a certain dollar limit, taxes and other special claims. Once all of these priority creditors are paid in full, general unsecured creditors are paid, and if there is any money left over claimants who do not timely file proofs of claim get some money. At the rock bottom are equity security holders—i.e., shareholders and members.

Bankruptcy Court *before* it and the Plan go out to creditors. Creditors are divided into classes. If there are different kinds of unsecured creditors, they will be divided into separate classes. Each secured creditor will usually be placed into a separate class. The Plan provides for "treatment" of each of the classes of creditors, unsecured and secured.

Each class votes on the treatment the Plan provides for that class. The Plan is confirmable if each class receives a majority in number and two-thirds in amount of affirmative votes. However, there is a procedure, called "cram-down"[128] that permits confirmation if at least one class votes affirmatively for the Plan, and the court finds that the treatment provided in the Plan is "fair and equitable."

"Fair and Equitable" is defined in the Bankruptcy Code differently for unsecured creditors and secured creditors. The determination of whether a *secured* class is treated in a fair and equitable manner may be quite complicated and could require an evidentiary hearing before the Bankruptcy Court.[129] On the other hand, the determination of whether the treatment of an *unsecured* class is fair and equitable is generally much simpler but could have a draconian result.

If the Debtor has to use the "cram-down" provision of Chapter 11 on an unsecured class, one very important rule which will then apply to the case is one which complicates many Chapter 11's. This rule is what is known as the *absolute priority rule*. The applicability of this rule is a shock to many business Chapter 11 debtors. The rule is applicable when the Plan is not accepted by all of the unsecured classes of creditors, and "cram-down" is the only way the plan can be confirmed. In that scenario if the unsecured classes which did not accept the Plan are not paid 100 % of their claims, the equity class, i.e., the stockholders or membership interest holders, cannot retain their ownership in the debtor after confirmation unless

---

128 "Cram-Down" is a phrase which has been used in the bankruptcy law for decades; but interestingly the phrase is found nowhere in the actual statute!

129 The provisions in the Bankruptcy Code dealing with cram-down of a secured class are too complicated for discussion in this Book.

they contribute new money to the debtor which can be used to pay the creditors. Thus, if the owners want to continue to own the company, they will have to contribute some additional consideration which can be used to pay the creditors. If that happens and is approved by the Bankruptcy Court, the owners' equity interests are essentially cancelled, and the debtor is essentially "sold" to the prior owners for the additional consideration. You can readily see how this could be expensive—and it is not a guaranteed result since other parties can also attempt to "buy" the debtor.

If the Chapter 11 Plan passes creditor muster or can be "crammed down," then it may be confirmed—i.e., the Plan goes into effect and is contractually and legally binding on the debtor and creditors—even those creditors who have voted against the plan—if the Court finds that it satisfies the other requirements of the Bankruptcy Code. Among the requirements are that creditors will receive consideration under the Plan which is at least as much as they would receive in a Chapter 7 liquidation; that the Plan is feasible; that the acceptance of the Plan was not solicited unlawfully; and that confirmation of the Plan is not going to be followed by a liquidation of the debtor unless that is what is contemplated under the Plan. There are a number of other requirements which are simply too complicated to be included here.

Sub-Chapter V of Chapter 11— A Special Option for Small Businesses

Until recently a Chapter 11 proceeding was really out of the financial reach of many small businesses. Several amendments to the small business section of Chapter 11 have made it less complex and cheaper for small businesses. Known as "Sub-Chapter V" (11 U.S.C. § 1181, *et seq*), it provides substantial benefits to small businesses. Sub-Chapter V resembles Chapter 12 (for farmers), discussed briefly in the prior chapter on bankruptcy and has some attributes of the consumer Chapter 13.

Originally, Sub-Chapter V was only available to a small business debtor which had debts not more than approximately $2.7 million. However, the CARES Act increased that amount to approximately $7.5 million, an amount which made Sub-Chapter V attractive to many troubled debtors. Note, however, that this increased limit only lasts for one year unless Congress decides to extend it. In a Sub-Chapter V, a Trustee having oversight and monitoring duties is appointed. The Trustee has the added duty of trying to get the debtor and creditors to agree to a consensual plan. The debtor, however, continues to be in possession of the debtor's assets and is permitted to conduct its business.

Sub-Chapter V makes the whole Chapter 11 process quicker and less complicated. However, it is still a legal process which requires a skilled bankruptcy lawyer's representation of the debtor. A Plan of Reorganization or liquidation is still required, but the process is greatly simplified. Although Sub-Chapter V doesn't require the filing of a Disclosure Statement, it does require the debtor to include background and other financial information in the Plan document. By adopting some Chapter 13 procedures, Sub-Chapter V makes it possible to confirm a Plan even if voted down by the creditors. Importantly, Sub-Chapter V does not include the draconian absolute priority rule, discussed above.

I must stress again that Chapter 11, whether regular Chapter 11 or Sub-Chapter V, will not culminate in a successful reorganization unless the debtor is viable, or the case is filed for the purpose of liquidating the company. Remember Chapter 11 is like *Hotel California*!

CHAPTER 12

OTHER CREDITORS' RIGHTS ISSUES

I have covered a lot of creditors' rights and debtor relief subjects in prior chapters. In this chapter I am going to discuss several other creditors' rights and debtor relief issues of a more specific nature which may be of interest to some small businesspeople.

Debt Buyers: A New Sheriff's in Town

Remember in Chapter 10 I told the story of the hotel I represented which had an "Interim Forbearance Agreement. The hotel's occupancy was not enough to satisfy the requirements of a lender which had offered permanent financing. The permanent lender therefore declined to take out the construction loan and left the construction lender "holding the bag."

As I related to you, we engaged in a workout which included trying to get the bank to give my client a discount in the amount owed so that we could either obtain some short-term financing from another bank or do a short sale[130] of the property to a buyer which had made an offer to purchase the hotel. The idea was to refinance or sell the property without having any lingering deficiency indebtedness owed to the bank. The bank would not

---

130 Most consumers know what a "short sale" is because they or someone they knew had to do one during the Great Recession. It works the same way in the commercial world. Real or personal property is sold with the secured lender's permission for *less* than what is owing to the lender.

agree, and it appeared that Chapter 11 might be the only remedy. Then one day my client called me and said he had gotten a letter from a new lender who said that it had purchased the loan from the bank.[131]

As indicated in our prior discussions, debt buyers have proliferated in our commercial economy in recent years. We have covered debt buyers which purchased loan portfolios previously owned by failed banks. These loan portfolios were purchased from the FDIC. It turns out that these same debt buyers and new ones are also in the business of buying bad debts from banks which are not in trouble, but simply are looking for an expedient way to get rid of bad loans in their portfolio.

Typically, the bank is engaged in a workout with the borrower and has concluded that it is not going to collect more than a certain amount of the loan. It is prepared to write the loan down on its books and take the loss. At that point it tries to find a debt buyer which will offer it a reasonable amount for the loan. Once the sale goes through, the bank writes off the loss, and the debt buyer steps into the shoes of the bank. Importantly, the borrower still owes the debt buyer the entire amount of the loan indebtedness—even though the debt buyer only paid less than 100 percent to the original bank, and possibly less than even 50 percent.

I have found in dealing with debt buyers that they are looking for one of two or maybe three possible results. First, many debt buyers—usually the smaller ones—are financing all or part of their loan purchase. *So, they have lenders, too!* These debt buyers typically want to get out of the loan quickly and make a profit. This means that if the borrower can refinance or sell the collateral quickly, the debt buyer will offer the borrower a nice, discounted pay-off. For example, suppose the debt buyer paid 50 cents on the dollar for the loan. It likely would offer a 25 percent discount for a quick pay-off. Remember, it is difficult in most cases to determine how much the debt buyer paid for the loan. They do not have to tell you,

---

131 We later found out through some "off the record discussions" with the old banker that the bank had sold the loan to the debt buyer for much less than the discount we had suggested to either refinance or sell the property. Go figure!

and generally unless you have some personal relationship with the original banker, he or she won't tell you either. However, many times in the workout negotiations you can get an approximate idea of what the discount was.

The second result is more draconian. The debt buyer wants to sell the collateral plus obtain some deficiency payment from the borrower. The fact that the borrower has hundreds of thousands of dollars, if not millions of dollars invested in the property makes no difference to the debt buyer. This is business, and empathy and equities don't apply! On the other hand, the borrower does have a small amount of leverage which can lead to either a waiver of any deficiency or at least payment of some reasonable amount which does not financially destroy the borrower or guarantors. That leverage is that the debt buyer cannot force the borrower to sell the property or to deed it over to the debt buyer. It's only recourse is to foreclose and sue the borrower and guarantors. Debt buyers are generally not interested in getting embroiled in litigation.[132]

I do not recommend that borrowers engage in negotiations with debt buyers without employing counsel. Representatives of debt buyers are generally quite skilled in what they do, and a borrower who does not have counsel is going to be at a great disadvantage.

There is a possible third result a debt buyer is seeking. This result happens from time to time. It is the situation where the debt buyer actually wants to own the collateral. For example, the debt buyer might be in the shopping center or office building business. The borrower's leverage is more important here because, as stated above, the debt buyer cannot force the borrower to transfer title to the property, and institution of foreclosure proceedings could take some time, and the borrower might also

---

132 An exception, of course, was with respect to some of the FDIC debt buyers who apparently enjoyed brutalizing borrowers with loans from failed banks.

file bankruptcy. My experience is that in this scenario, there is more like-lihood that a deed in lieu of foreclosure[133] and little or no deficiency could be negotiated.

The Management/Sale Scheme

Anyone who owns a financially troubled company knows how many calls and emails they get from lawyers and others who want to offer "help" in the form of workout advice or bankruptcy filings. Usually, these calls and emails start after a creditor files suit since the suit is on the public records. These people simply review the court filings for the names of trou-bled companies.

In one type of scheme, a troubled company might receive a call from a person who identifies himself as a representative of a company who wants to purchase the business. The prospective buyer meets with the owner of the troubled company and tells the owner that the company needs to be stabilized first, and then the buyer will purchase it. The proposal is that the buyer will take over management of the company, inject some capital and then buy the company for a certain agreed upon amount after so many days or months.

What actually happens is that these people get into the company, do not pay any of the bills of the company, do not inject new capital and steal the revenue of the company. They are generally gone before the owner of the company can find out what it is happening.

That is not to say that all buyers who propose management deals are crooks. Far from it. It may be that a company is on the verge of closing down. It needs capital to survive and probably a new business plan. A buyer wants to purchase the company, but there are legitimate business reasons why the buyer can't make an immediate purchase. For example, suppose the business has a government issued license, and under government

---

133 A deed in lieu of foreclosure is a deed from the owner of the property to the lender in either full or partial satisfaction of the debt.

regulations any change in ownership voids the license. It might take a number of months to obtain issuance of a new license for the buyer.

What is important, if you are approached by someone with this type of proposal, is to first employ a commercial lawyer who understands creditors' rights and debtor relief issues to help you determine if the buyer is for real and to properly document the transaction. Make sure the buyer has the financial backing and experience he needs to manage and purchase.

UCC Article 2 Sales Issues

In prior chapters I have discussed the Uniform Commercial Code. As I stated, the UCC governs commercial law in **all** of our states except for Louisiana which has a "civil"[134] law system but has at least enacted some of the UCC articles. Puerto Rico which also has a civil law system has also not enacted all of the articles. The statute as enacted in **most** states is virtually the same.[135]

I would imagine that most people reading this Book are small businesspeople. Many small businesses sell products as opposed to providing services. Article 2 of the UCC deals solely with the sale of products. Some of the rules set forth in Article 2 are complicated, but many represent the usual practices of merchants in most industries. The importance of Article 2 to creditors' rights issues is that Article 2 can and does govern issues of liability of a merchant buyer from a merchant seller or vendor.

Creation of the Contract of Sale

Article 2 of the UCC establishes how a contract of sale is created between the buyer and the seller or vendor. The usual scenario involves

---

134 "Civil Law" as used here means a legal system derived from the European systems mainly based on statutes as compared with the English system of law which forty-nine of our states and the District of Columbia use which is based on case law and also what is called the "common law."

135 There are differences, and advice on these differences needs to be given by a competent commercial lawyer.

some type of writing. However, many orders for goods are done orally. Section 2-201 of the UCC limits the enforceability of oral contracts to amounts or value of goods of $500.00 or less. That means that if a merchant places a small order of $500.00 or less through a telephone call, neither the buyer nor seller will be able to enforce the contract in court if there is some dispute.

You may wonder whether this really happens. It really doesn't because there is always some writing even though you don't realize it. If a buyer is a continuing customer of a particular vendor, and the sales are on credit, the buyer will have likely signed a credit application which will specify all of the terms governing the sales transactions with the vendor. Since most buyers never read these terms, you might be surprised how these terms affect your rights regarding return of non-conforming goods and other common occurrences. You also might be surprised to learn that you have unintentionally personally guaranteed the debt to the vendor.

If you simply go to the vendor's store and purchase the goods there, you will likely have to sign an order form or invoice, and that will contain all of the terms of the sale. As you can see, there is usually some sort of writing involved in virtually every commercial sales transactions.

In the usual transaction involving the purchase of goods, however, a buyer may send a "purchase order" to the vendor in which he orders a certain quantity of a certain type of product to be delivered to a certain place for a certain price. If you are a merchant buyer, you need to make sure your "purchase order" accurately and fully sets forth the quantity and description of the goods you are ordering and the price, credit terms and where it is to be delivered. This should not be a problem because you will already have ascertained all of that information through communications with the vendor prior to your order. However, it is also a good idea to include other terms if the goods are of a specialized nature.

One of the least understood sections of Article 2 by merchants is section 2-207. Section 2-207 attempts to resolve the problem which occurs when a written offer is made to purchase goods by a merchant from a vendor—usually by purchase order—and the vendor sends back a writing—usually an invoice—with terms and conditions not contained in the purchase order, or terms that are contrary to the terms and conditions in the purchase order.

Simply stated, section 2-207 provides that where the purchase order says that new terms proposed by the seller will not be accepted; the new proposed terms *materially alter* the terms proposed in the purchase offer; or where the buyer objects in writing to the new terms, **the new terms will not become part of the contract**. Otherwise, the terms proposed by the seller do become part of the contract. The words, "materially alter" are legal terms and have been construed by the courts to mean that the new terms would "surprise" the other party or would create a "hardship" on the other party.

So here is an example of what we are talking about. Suppose the purchase agreement from the buyer specifies the quantity, description, price and credit terms of the purchase. In our hypothetical the purchase order says that the buyer is purchasing 1,000 yellow, right-handed widgets for $10 per widget on 120-day credit terms. The buyer sends the purchase order to the vendor which ships the goods with an invoice which sets new credit terms of 90 days. Under UCC 2-207 this would constitute a "material alteration" of the terms of the purchase order and would not become part of the contract unless accepted by the buyer.

On the other hand, suppose the buyer's residence is Georgia and the vendor is in New York, and the invoice says that any dispute between the parties will be construed under New York law and litigated in New York. There is no doubt that the buyer's presumption is that if there is a dispute, it would be handled in the Georgia Courts. Is the vendor's invoice provision enforceable? Has the vendor made a material alteration? Courts are split on whether venue for litigation constitutes a material alteration. It just depends on the facts of each case.

How does a buyer keep this type of problem from occurring? It's simple. Put *all* of the terms and conditions in your purchase order. If the seller/vendor is out of state or out of the country, put a provision in the purchase order that says that your state's law governs, and that any dispute will be resolved in the courts of your state and that no change to venue is acceptable. You should also put language in the purchase order that terms not set forth in the purchase order will not be accepted. You will have then neutralized any changes which might appear in the seller/vendor's invoice or other paperwork. If the seller objects, you can work out the issue with him or her. If there is no objection, you have neutralized any change in venue or other terms.

Course of Dealing or Performance

Using what we have learned about the creation of the contract of sale, what if the parties do not follow one or more of the written terms. Here is another hypothetical. Suppose that both the purchase order and the invoice from the seller cover the purchase and sale of 10,000 widgets with 1,000 widgets being shipped each month for ten months. Both the purchase order and the acceptance by the seller/vendor provide for payment to be made within 30 days of the receipt of each monthly shipment. However, the "course of performance" by the parties is different. The buyer pays for each shipment 60 days after each shipment is received, and the seller accepts the payment and does not object to the different terms. Does the "course of performance" modify the contract between the parties?

First of all, state courts differ in how they construe "course of performance." So, if a dispute occurs between you and a vendor, you are best advised to seek legal advice from an attorney who is skilled in the commercial law of your particular state. That said, many courts construe the UCC provisions governing this scenario as creating a "waiver" of the credit terms so that the parties have essentially waived the requirement of a 30-day payment. However, importantly, the seller can always rescind the waiver by giving notice that the next payment must be made in 30 days.

"Course of Dealing" is not the same as "Course of Performance" and cannot result in a waiver. Course of Dealing under the UCC means how the parties perform in a sequence of *different* transactions occurring over time rather than how they perform in *one* transaction. In our hypothetical, although the contract covered ten shipments and payments, it was still just one contract.

No small business buyer or seller wants to litigate anything. Lawyers are expensive, and courts and juries are unpredictable. The best advice is to put all the terms of a sales contract in the paperwork between the parties and to perform under those terms. If terms need to be changed, simply do it in writing!

Alter Ego Litigation

It seems in recent times that creditors are seeking more innovative ways of crushing their debtors in litigation. If the creditor for whatever reason does not have a guarantee of the principals of the small business debtor,[136] the creditor may allege in the litigation that the owners of the debtor are *alter egos* of the borrower and therefore, in reality, the borrower and the owners are one and the same. The creditor is said to be requesting that the court *pierce the corporate veil* of the entity and get to the owners.

In my practice I have seen these *alter ego* cases result in the financial ruination of the owner of the company. I believe the reason for this even being an issue is that small businesspeople are not careful in how they internally manage their corporate entities— whether the entity is a corporation or limited liability company. State case law defines what is necessary to create the *alter ego* claim. One state court has called it "an *equitable doctrine* which is used to disregard the separate and distinct legal existence possessed by a corporation where it is established that the corporation served as a mere

---

136 Usually this is not a bank creditor because it is quite uncommon for a bank not to require a personal guarantee from its small business borrowers.

alter ego or *business conduit* of another."[137] Importantly, the *alter ego* doctrine can also result in two affiliate companies being the *alter ego* of the other. This happens sometimes in a family business in which there are a number of different entities created, but they are all treated as one company.[138]

To prove an *alter ego* case or to *pierce the corporate veil* courts generally require evidence that the owners disregarded the separateness of the entities by not keeping separate records, commingling assets and confusing the otherwise separate entities so that the entities are just a subterfuge. There is also the requirement that some injustice occur as a result of the lack of separateness. In other words, the concept of *piercing the corporate veil* does not exist simply to penalize a debtor and to provide a windfall for the creditor who does not have a personal guarantee, but instead provides a remedy for a creditor when an owner (or other entity) abuses the separate corporate entity by using it as a piggy bank or unlawfully which has the effect of harming the creditor.

A good example of an *alter ego* case is as follows. Suppose Jack and Jill Pierce create a company to sell bridal veils. They call it the Pierce Bridal Veil Co., Inc. Business is good, and Jack and Jill decide to let the company pay for their cars, their insurance, the mortgage on their house and they pull out cash on a weekly basis—other than their salaries—for personal use. Their two kids, Hughie and Dewey, are in college, and Jack and Jill have them on the payroll of the company so that the kids can use their salaries to pay for their room and board at college. The kids do not really work at Pierce Bridal. From time-to-time Jack and Jill charge personal purchases to the company credit card.

Their main creditor is Veil Manufacturing Company which manufactures the bridal veils which Pierce Bridal sells. Veil did not get a personal

---

137 Although probably unnecessary since this Book is not a treatise, I do want to give a cite for this quote: *Kissun v. Humana, Inc.,* 267 Ga. 419 (Supreme Court of Georgia, 1997).

138 For example, suppose the business consists of an operating company, a company which owns a warehouse used by the operating company, and a company which owns the equipment used in the business operation. If the owners do not treat these as separate and distinct entities, there is the possibility of an *alter ego* case if the business suffers financial difficulties.

guarantee from Jack or Jill. Suppose that due to the Covid Pandemic, weddings are down significantly, and Jack and Jill have taken so much money out of Pierce Bridal, that the company is no longer viable and can't pay its debt to Veil. Pierce Bridal defaults and goes out of business. Veil sues it and obtains a judgment. It then files an *alter ego* case against Jack and Jill.

It is easy to see from these extreme facts that Jack and Jill have disregarded the corporate separateness of Pierce Bridal and, importantly, that this disregard has worked an injustice on, and has harmed Veil, i.e., Veil can't get paid the debt owed by Pierce Bridal. Thus, had Jack and Jill not drained Pierce Bridal for their own personal use, it would have assets available which could have been used to pay Veil.

The rule to follow is simple. If you are going to use a corporate entity (corporation, limited liability company, limited liability partnership, etc.), make sure you treat it as a separate entity and not as your personal piggy bank.

The Independent Director

I wondered if I should even cover the "Independent Director" in my Book; but I decided to do so because of the potential harm it can cause to a small business. As explained by example below, I found it incredible that a lender would have the "chutzpah"/gall to require a small business borrower to appoint an independent director, and that anyone would have the guts to serve as one. That said, there is no question that when and if this happens to a small business, it can be extremely harmful.

I would dare say that very few readers and possibly commercial practitioners have seen the fact situation that I am about to describe. Suppose a business has a substantial loan with the bank. The business has had a string of financial difficulties, and the bank has determined that the loan cannot be refinanced and that working out the loan is the only solution. During the workout the bank wants to be able to control the money flow and the activities of the borrower and essentially bleed out the borrower by liquidating the borrower's assets while continuing some semblance of the borrower staying in business. The bank does not want to "waste" any of the borrower's revenues on payments to unsecured vendors. However, in order to keep the borrower operating it may allow some payments to those creditors who will not supply the borrower with necessary inventory or raw materials unless they are paid.

A bankruptcy filing would adversely affect the bank's strategy and actions and cede control back to the business as debtor in possession. While a bankruptcy would likely be good for the borrower and any guarantors and probably for the borrower's other creditors, it would not be good for the bank.

In order to protect itself against the borrower filing bankruptcy, the bank requires the borrower to appoint an independent director (or manager in the case of a limited liability company). The bank also requires the borrower to amend its by-laws (or operating agreement) to provide that it takes a unanimous vote of the directors or managers to approve the filing of a bankruptcy. Thus, unless the independent director/manager votes to permit the bankruptcy filing, the debtor cannot file bankruptcy.[139]

Without getting into an in-depth analysis of the law on this issue, I can tell you that any lender who insists on these provisions is risking a lender liability case if the filing of the bankruptcy would have a positive effect on the debtor and its other creditors. The same is also true of the independent director who may incur a substantial risk of liability.[140] These are draconian provisions and should be resisted by borrowers and guarantors.

---

139 Entities must have authorization from their board of directors, partners or members in order to file bankruptcy. Their by-laws, partnership agreement or operating agreement determines what the requisite majority is for such authorization.

140 Several years ago, I represented a company which had an independent director forced upon the company by its lender. Apparently, the independent director had created a nice business for himself and was known by a number of lenders as someone who would always vote against filing a bankruptcy. When I told the independent director that we were going to file anyway, and that if he aided the bank in trying to get the bankruptcy case dismissed, he would be sued, he resigned. Perhaps my suggesting that his actions would be in bad faith and perhaps not covered by the company's directors and officers liability insurance contributed to his decision to resign!

In our discussion in the guarantor chapter of this Book, I mentioned "bad-boy (girl)" guarantees. Most of these types of guarantee agreements, make the voluntary filing of a bankruptcy petition a trigger under the guarantee which makes the guarantor liable for the entire debt. This, of course, has a similar result of restricting the filing of bankruptcy as in the independent director scenario—except that the guarantor can actually still file the bankruptcy where a company with an independent director cannot.

If the bank is requiring you to appoint an independent director, you need to immediately employ an attorney with commercial law experience to advise you.

Foreclosing Equity Interests

Some banks and other lenders require that the owners of a borrower pledge their ownership equity interests in the borrower as collateral for their guarantee obligations. Thus, if the borrower is a corporation, the owners' stock would be pledged to the lender. If the borrower is an LLC, it would be the owners' membership interests which are pledged to the lender. A hybrid form of this is for the lender not to take as security interest in the actual stock or membership interest, but to take an assignment of the voting rights of the owners.

It is one thing for a lender to take a security interest in the equity interests; it is entirely another thing for the lender to actually foreclose the equity interests or to vote the equity interests. It is difficult to see why a lender would want to take ownership or control of a troubled borrower. The logic against such an action by the lender is obvious. The troubled borrower will likely have numerous other creditors who could be affected by the lender's actions in operating the company.

Usually, the lender's purpose in taking control is to make sure that it will be first to be paid out of the borrower's assets—to the possible detriment of the other creditors. However, another possible reason would be to take ownership of the borrower's business. As indicated elsewhere in our discussions, I have seen debt buyers who are really looking to own the collateral and actually begin foreclosing the equity interests. If they are successful, the debt buyer will be in the untenable position of having a security interest in most, if not all of the borrower's assets *and* ownership of the stock or membership interests. In my view this is simply an invitation for a lender liability suit by the borrower and probably creditors.

Nevertheless, I still occasionally see lenders take pledges of the guarantors' ownership interests. My suggestion is for guarantors to avoid permitting the lender to do this, or if the lender insists, to negotiate a bad boy/girl guarantee in consideration for the pledge.

CONCLUSION

We have covered a lot of territory in this Book. In my conclusion I want to summarize some important rules and concepts which I have addressed. But I also want to suggest changes in state and federal laws which will level the playing field for borrowers and guarantors from the steep incline of today to what I believe is the appropriate "somewhat uphill," but fairer treatment of borrowers and guarantors.

Summary

1. Never let your spouse or another family member guarantee a loan or other credit extension unless they are involved in a significant way in the business and have an independent financial strength necessary to obtain the credit. Even then, resist as forcefully as you can.

2. Never pledge your personal residence to secure a guarantee, or to borrow money to put into your business unless you are sure that the business has plenty of free and clear assets to pay off any borrowings—which in a startup is unlikely. If you have to pledge your personal residence, try to negotiate a deal in which the lender agrees to liquidate the company's assets first and your residence last.

3. Never provide a personal guarantee or pledge your own personal property to secure a troubled loan. Make the bank work it out with you without putting your financial life at risk.

4. Always try to negotiate a "bad boy/bad girl" guarantee or at least cap the guarantee at an amount that will not drive you into bankruptcy; or negotiate a "sunset" guarantee which reduces over a period of time until it is gone. If the bank is not sophisticated enough to know what a "bad boy/bad girl" guarantee is, or has some internal rules against them, find another bank.

5. Prior to borrowing money from the bank, the borrower (and guarantors) need to do four very important things: first, consider how the structure of the loan will affect the business' finances and the finances of the guarantors if the business defaults in the loan. Secondly, read all of the loan papers, even if the banker tells you that the bank will not "change a word" in any of them. Thirdly, look objectively as you can at your business. Is the business really viable? Is the intended use of the loan proceeds really necessary, or will they be used to finance a "pipe dream?" Finally, be prepared to walk away from the bank's proposal and find another lender.

6. If your business has defaulted and is in a workout with the bank, do not liquidate the assets for the bank except as part of a negotiated settlement of the deficiency. Remember, a guarantor has a little leverage in the beginning of the workout, but no leverage once the business assets are liquidated.

7. Negotiate with the SBA bank and be prepared to find another lender if you can't get the structure you want. Remember that there are some parts of the SBA loan structure that are negotiable and others that are not. Never pledge your personal residence. Walk away if the bank insists. Remember that in the event your business doesn't make it, the government can take whatever personal assets you have, including your personal residence; and there is no statute of limitations on the "offset" ability of the government. The SBA is not your friend, even though the SBA lender appears to be.

8. Chapter 7 is usually not warranted for a financially troubled "entity" which is going out of business. Filing one will open up every closet and expose every skeleton.

9. Chapter 11 is an absolutely last resort. Do not let anyone tell you that it is easy, and if it doesn't work out you can get out of it. Remember *Hotel California*!

10. Avoid personally guaranteeing vendor debt. Read every credit application carefully. If you have to guarantee the debt, negotiate a "sunset" provision or a cap.

11. Use a form purchase order when engaging in any significant purchase of goods or services. Put your own fine print in the purchase order, including a statement that your business does not agree to any additional terms not in the purchase order unless they are "expressly" approved by the buyer.

12. If you are a contractor, follow the same rules I have suggested above for the structure of a bank loan in your dealings with a surety. If the bond covers a significant undertaking, make sure that your company is viable enough to take on such a project. If you can, avoid signing any "pay when paid" contract. Construction law and practice is a specialty, and construction law differs from one state to another. Employ a competent lawyer who specializes in construction law if you have any doubt about the structure of the construction or surety contracts you are asked to sign.

13. Finally, stay away from Independent Directors.

Suggested Changes in the Law

Throughout this Book I have discussed some of the unfair federal and state laws governing creditors' rights and debtor relief. I have said many times that borrowers don't have a lobby in Congress or in state legislatures. As soon as a legislator introduces a bill which might help small businesses and their owners, the bank/creditor lobby begins to yell and scream that it will harm the ability of small businesses to get credit. That is simply bull. Small business lending (not just SBA lending) is a major part of banking. The banks will not leave a state because of a few laws which protect small businesses and their owners.

Here are a few suggested changes, some of which may already be the law in your particular state:

1. Every state should either adopt some form of Tenants by the Entirety so that at the very least a borrower's personal residence will not be subject to judgment liens. In fact, in our modern society where people do not always get married and live together, any dual

joint ownership of a residence should be protected by TBE if both people live in the residence.

2. A reasonable homestead exemption—i.e., an exemption from judgment liens and levies— should be available to everyone, whether married, head of the household or single. It should include equity of up to $1 million in a residence and $100,000.00 of consumer household goods and vehicles. It is just outrageous for judgment creditors to be able to take a person's house and consumer household goods.

3. Wage garnishment should be outlawed nationwide, and wages should retain their "character" once deposited into the debtor's bank accounts so that they cannot be garnished by a creditor who garnishes the debtor's bank account. This already is the law in several states.

4. The statute of limitations on credit card debt should be limited to four years, and some consideration should be given to stop the trafficking in sales of credit card debt to unscrupulous debt buyers. This could be easily done by limiting the recovery by the assignee to whatever was paid for the debt.

5. Bankruptcy law should be amended to permanently increase the "Sub-Chapter V" debt limit to $10 million and increase the affiliate aggregate to $15 million.[141]

6. Collection of government debts, whether of tax or SBA origin should be limited to ten years from the date of assessment

---

141 Sub-Chapter V contains a provision which effectively prohibits affiliates of debtors (the owners, brother-sister companies, etc.) from filing bankruptcy if the aggregate non-insider debt owed by those filing exceeds the small business maximum.

regarding taxes, and the date the borrower defaulted in regard to SBA and other government debts.

7. Deficiencies should be barred in non-judicial foreclosures of commercial mortgages unless the foreclosing lender obtains court validation of the lender's foreclosure bid price. If the non-judicial foreclosure occurs after suit is filed against the borrower or guarantors, any judgment recovered should not be enforceable if the creditor later proceeds to non-judicial foreclosure until the value of the foreclosed real estate is determined by the court and deducted from the judgment amount. Waivers of these rights should be unenforceable.[142]

8. Deficiencies should be barred on any foreclosure of a purchase money mortgage on a borrower's personal residence.

9. The Uniform Commercial Code should be amended so that waivers of notices and the commercial reasonableness of a sale of collateral cannot be waived by a borrower or guarantors.

10. The laws governing the "Statute of Frauds" insofar as it applies to personal guarantees should be strengthened so that no evidence outside of the "four corners" of the guarantee should be admissible in evidence against a guarantor, and the guarantor should not be required to waive the defense of violating the statute of frauds. Most personal guarantees use the lender or vendor's form. If the bank or other creditor is sloppy in filling out a personal guarantee form, the creditor should suffer the consequence of the guarantee being unenforceable. Courts in many states are allowing testimonial evidence, emails and other evidence to shore up the liability of the guarantor. Let's level the playing field a bit.

---

142 North Carolina has a similar statute, and waivers are not enforceable.

11. There should be some government regulation, probably on the federal level, of the new online high yield lenders, i.e., those charging credit card rates of 30 % or more.

I would like to make a final observation. I have never believed that the law on creditors' rights and debtor relief should be a Democrat or Republican, blue state or red state issue. Perhaps it is in some places, but it really is a function of basic fairness in commercial and consumer matters. It is certainly true that old line Republicans want less governmental regulation, while old line Democrats like more regulation.[143] We have seen in this Book that a number of very red states have TBE laws and have enacted other laws which protect commercial and consumer borrowers alike from predatory lending. A number of Republican states also do not allow wage garnishment or basically any garnishment at all except against commercial bank accounts. It is so interesting to me that in these "red" states there has never been any serious attempt to repeal these laws.

It seems to me that perhaps a number of the legislators in these states have recognized that they themselves are small businessmen and women and that they also have to personally guarantee loans with banks just as their constituents—and they realize that these laws benefit them, too! What comes around, goes around!

---

143 I'm not sure where the new ultra-liberal Democrats and ultra conservative Republicans come out on these issues.

ACKNOWLEDGMENTS AND THANKS

Writing this Book has been a multi-year project. I coined the title at least a decade ago. If anything good has come from Covid for me, it is that I had time at home to finish it. I could not have written this Book without the encouragement and help from my wife, Patty, who for many years, besides being a mother to our three sons and taking care of me, was also my bankruptcy paralegal.

I also thank my now retired partner of 35 years, Karen Fagin White, Esquire, who gave me many well-taken suggestions and criticisms. My partners, Brent Herrin, Esquire, Anna Humnicky, Esquire, and Ben Klehr, Esquire, also gave me suggestions and help. Brent, besides being a commercial litigator, has a specialty in tax and reviewed by comments in this Book on tax law. My paralegal of over 30 years, Karla Lemons, who knows as much commercial law and procedure as many lawyers did the final editing and proofreading which was quite a task. Our firm's long-time legal assistant, Lara Carlton, who is a guru in Microsoft Word, was of great help in figuring out how to correct what I thought were "uncorrectable" errors. Thanks to all of them!

Finally, although I have personally mentored a number of lawyers over the years, I also have had mentors. Sam Zusmann, now retired in Orlando, and the late Morris Macey significantly helped shape my career. The Honorable Stacey Cotton, a retired Atlanta Bankruptcy Judge, helped me enormously in the early 1980's after I went out on my own and before he went on the bench. Finally, thanks so much to the first bankruptcy judge I ever appeared before over fifty years ago, Judge W. Homer Drake (now retired). Judge Drake is one of the true giants in the bankruptcy legal community of this country and helped me so much in my career.

GHS